Is Financial Prosperity for Us Today or the Thousand-Year Reign of Jesus Christ?

12 Biblical Truths Concerning Financial Prosperity

Allen J. Charbonnet, Sr.

XULON
PRESS

Is Financial Prosperity for Us Today or the Thousand-Year Reign of Jesus Christ?
by Allen J. Charbonnet Sr.
p. cm.

Printed in the United States of America

ISBN 1-60034-494-1

Library of Congress Cataloging-in-Publication Data

www.xulonpress.com

CONTENTS

Introduction

In 1975 God poured out upon me four miracles, and I don't believe God gives miracles for no reason. There is a fullness of time for everything; I believe that this book has something to do with those miracles. This book that I have written is called *Is Financial Prosperity for Us Today or the Thousand-Year Reign of Jesus Christ?* The word "thousand" means millennium. I asked three Christians what did the word "millennium" mean in reference to the Bible, and I went zero for three. So I thought, I won't say millennium but say a thousand, since they mean the same. Now I should get three out of three, right? So when I ask someone what the thousand-year reign of Jesus Christ means, everyone should know.

I didn't want to put the word "millennium" in this book and no one or a very few people would know what it means. So it is called "Financial Prosperity Today." Today is today, which means the time we are living in now, or is it in the thousand-year reign of Jesus?

There are <u>twelve biblical truths that the Holy Spirit revealed to me</u>. How do I know that it was the Holy Spirit who revealed this to me? It is 100 percent scriptural, that's why, and it is far above my natural wisdom. You need to read this for yourself, in your Bible, which I will show you. I did not say twelve Scriptures; I said twelve Bible truths that will contain hundreds of Scriptures with chapter and verses. These are all truths, and you can look them up in your Bible; I am going to show you where they are.

Now the reason I am teaching this is because the Holy Spirit revealed this to me in the year 2002. However, I was not yet ready to write this book because I was angry about what was being taught; it just did not measure up to the Bible. Today God has released me, because I can write with a heart of love and with the right motive to edify the body of Christ.

This book is written not to accuse anyone of heresy, No! No! No! There are major doctrines like Jesus is God, salvation thru faith, the Trinity, the virgin birth, bodily resurrection, Jesus is the Messiah, etc, that constitute serious heresy. My intent is not to call people heretics, false prophets, or false apostles, but to reveal something that today we may be greatly missing—the fullness of God's time concerning material riches in the Scriptures. Now, the reason I am showing you these Scriptures is this: when the early church had a disagreement, they came together and brought out the testimonies of what God had showed them, then they made a decision. So the Holy Spirit has revealed these twelve truths to me from the Scriptures to reveal to the body of Christ, the church. <u>I challenge you to read the whole book and seriously study the Scriptures that the Holy Spirit showed me, and then you can make your own judgment.</u>

You can make a decision concerning the prosperity finances; is it speaking about today, our time, or the thousand-year reign of Jesus? Let me say that I definitely believe God wants to meet all your needs today, as shown in Philippians 4:19. However, the teachings that we can all be rich like Abraham, Solomon, etc, are not Bible truths, because they are not Scripture. *Remember read the entire book* before making your decision. Just about all those who teach this kind of prosperity use almost all Old Testament Scriptures. I deal with this in Truth # 3. You will see the difference between the Old Testament and the New Testament concerning the true riches of God. *Don't think we cannot miss God's timing, remember Israel was looking for the Lion of Judah to come and set up his earthly kingdom.* Jesus came as the Lamb of God to redeem mankind from their sins. Israel missed the time of His visitation; I believe we are missing God's timing concerning finances now, today, our time, or is it the thousand-year reign of Jesus Christ?

What is being preached is right, but the Scriptures (twelve Bible truths) prove the timing is wrong. No one has it all right, although many preachers would like to believe they do. Today, we are rejecting the teaching and preaching of men of the past, as if we have some great wisdom and revelation above all the previous ministers of God concerning financial prosperity. The men of old preached spiritual values as holiness and hell—damnation, but today mostly we hear is about is material values, a lot of prosperity preaching on how God wants us to be rich. I was taught this also as a young Christian and a young pastor; but as time when on, and as I studied the Scriptures in detail, I began to see that was not what the Bible was really saying. The more I look for Scriptures to validate the financial prosperity teaching, the more the Spirit of God would point me to scripture after scripture revealing the opposite. Then I got to a place of *no return based on the Scriptures*. So I had to be quiet, not emotional, not jumping up and down claiming stuff and all kinds of wealth.

<u>Relax, read, be quiet, and keep your cool</u>—<u>not being emotional, read the entire book.</u> I didn't write this book out of anger or to condemn anyone, but to reveal what the Holy Spirit revealed to me. I believe this is what God has revealed to me for the present time to reveal to His church. There are a lot of teachings about financial prosperity/riches that are not Scripture. Preachers are saying certain things because other preachers teach and say certain things that are totally unscriptural. They are not searching the Scriptures for themselves in detail.

CHAPTER 1

Search the Scriptures

When the Bible speaks about *problems* that occurred in the church, it says that *they came together* (Acts 15:2, 6) *to solve the problem,* to discuss the matter, and to search the Scriptures for the answer. In John 5:39, <u>Jesus said, "Search the scriptures</u> for in them you think . . ." So what we are going to do is search the Scriptures, for we think. In Acts 17:11 Paul went down to Berea and the people were more noble (open-minded) and wiser than the people of Thessalonica, for <u>they searched the Scriptures daily</u> to see if what Paul was telling them was true or not. 2 Timothy 3:16 says, "All scripture is given by inspiration of God and is profitable for doctrine, for reproof, for correction, for instruction in righteousness."

Let us look at Acts chapter 15; I will cover certain key verses. Verse 1: certain men said that the Gentiles were to be circumcised after the law of Moses; however, we know that was done away within Christ. Therefore, Paul and Barnabas had a major disagreement with them. There was a great debate, in other words a great discussion, concerning this matter. Now they got together and determined that Paul, Barnabas, and certain others should go up to Jerusalem. "And certain men which came down from Judea taught the brethren, and said, Except you be circumcised after the manner of Moses, ye cannot be saved." Certain Jews wanted the apostles and elders to consider this matter and see what God had to say about it. They weren't calling each other heretics.

Acts 15:5 says, "But there rose up certain of the sect of the Pharisees which believed, saying, That it was needful to circumcise them, and to command them to keep the law of Moses." Verse 6: *"And the apostles and elders came together for to consider of this matter."* They weren't calling each other heretics, false apostles, false elders, false this or false that, but considering the matter. Only Jesus has it all together, 100 percent all the time, not Paul, not Peter, nor John, and definitely not us today, only Jesus.

In 1 Corinthians 3:1-4, Paul calls the Corinthians carnal Christians, like babes in Christ, because they were walking in strife and division. Acts 15:7 says: "And when there had been much disputing, Peter rose up, and said unto them, Men and brethren, ye know how that a good while ago God made choice among us, that the Gentiles by my mouth should hear the words of the gospel, and believe." Verse 8: "And God, which knoweth the hearts, bare them witness, giving them the Holy Ghost, even as He did unto us." Verse 9: "And put no difference between us and them, purifying their hearts by faith." As they were discussing this matter, he goes on to say in verse 10, "Now therefore why tempt ye God, to put a yoke upon the neck of the disciples, which neither our fathers nor we were able to bear?" Then he said in verse 11, "But we believe that through the grace of the Lord Jesus Christ we shall be saved, even as they."

Verse 12: "Then all the multitude kept silence . . ." — kept what? They kept silent; they were neither emotional nor jumping up and down. Why do I bring this up? Because <u>many Christians are very emotional when they hear about money,</u> and if we get all emotional we won't know what the Bible is truly saying. Another problem we have in this area is that we have one group teaching that God wants us to be rich and the other group teaches that we should be poor. God wants our needs met, which means the focus is neither on rich nor poor.

In Acts 17:11, Paul speaks about the people of Berea being more noble than the people of Thessalonica. The people of Thessalonica didn't study the Scriptures in detail, but allowed their emotions to control them. They ran Paul out of town (Acts 17:5,10). What's happening today is that *many of today's preachers and Christians are listening to what someone else is saying, and they are saying the same*. They are not really studying the Scriptures in detail for themselves. For example, did you not know that the word "prosper" in 3 John 2 is the only place in the New Testament that that word appears? Acts 2:1 thru Revelation 3:22; 3,816 verses, the entire church age that we live in today. I will deal with the word "prosper" (3 John 2) in Truth # 4.

Once I received a book concerning financial prosperity from a sister in the Lord, whom my ministry still supports. She said she was not used to writing books about finances, so she was stepping out by faith by writing this book. She said I am using the same Scriptures as others, so this is my chance to write a book on finances, to get out there and join the crowd, as one would say. NO! NO! NO! You don't join anything because of others; you have to search the Scriptures yourself, as Jesus said in John 5:39. In 2 Timothy 2:18, some were saying that the resurrection had already passed. Even in the days of the apostle Paul, some were missing the truth of the Scriptures. This is not something new or unusual. Acts 15:13 says, "And after they had held their peace, James answered, saying, Men and brethren, hearken unto me." They began to listen; verse 14: "Simeon hath declared how God at the first did visit the Gentiles, to take out of them a people for his name." Verse 15: "And to this agree the words of the prophets; *as it is written.*" Written where? It is written in the Scriptures. Remember Jesus says in John 5:39, "Search the scriptures; for in them ye think . . ." He was telling the Jews if they thought they had eternal life, they had better search the Scriptures.

Acts 17:11, They were more noble because they searched the Scriptures daily, so we shouldn't just get on the bandwagon because the bandwagon is going north and everyone else is jumping on it. Many men of old—40-50 plus years ago—taught that the principal and most important thing is our lifestyle, to live for God, a spiritual life of holiness, serving the Lord with all our hearts. Now I am not telling you that God wants you broke and in poverty, because the Bible says in Philippians 4:19, "My God shall supply all your need . . ." It is in moderation, neither rich nor poor. You can agree or disagree, but I will show you in these twelve bible truths that God's true riches are spiritual things. In the New Testament, God did not focus on financial nor material things.

In Acts 15:16 thru 18, James was quoting the Scriptures; he was telling the multitude what the Scriptures were saying. That's why we must look into the Scriptures. God called me into a teaching ministry (Eph. 4:11 and 1 Cor. 12:28). I constantly search the Scriptures in detail. In 2 Thessalonians 2:1 thru 3, men were saying that the rapture had already occurred. Verse 3: *Paul says "Let no man deceive you* by any means: for that day shall not come, except there come a falling away first, and that man of sin be revealed, the son of perdition." That's the Antichrist. He hasn't come yet. They were telling the Christians that the rapture had already happened. This is why Paul wrote concerning this matter, explaining to them this had not yet occurred and they were in error. They were too soon, the timing was off, about 2,000 years plus off, just as I believe that we are with the prosperity/riches teachings. 2 Thessalonians 2:5: "Remember ye not, that when I was yet with you, I told you those things?" Verse 8 tells us that when "that Wicked be revealed, whom the Lord shall consume with the spirit of his mouth, and shall destroy with the brightness of his coming." That's when the thousand-year reign of Jesus Christ (Rev. 20:4) shall begin, and Jesus shall reign on this earth for a thousand years and we shall reign with him on the earth.

Revelation 5:10 states that *we shall reign on the earth, that's when the saints shall possess the financial riches of the heathen* (Truth #1). We are rich now, spiritually, beginning with the new birth. I want to challenge you to read this book and its entire twelve Bible truths. Search out each verse of Scripture in the Bible.

CHAPTER 2

Truth # 1:

Jesus Never Promised That Every Christian Could Be Rich, a Millionaire, or Have an Abundance of Money in This Age

The Holy Spirit revealed this truth to me so that many believers won't have any false hope. This truth is revealed in Matthew 19:27-30. However, let's start with Mark 10:28. "Then Peter began to say unto him, Lo, we have left all, and have followed thee." Verse 29: "And Jesus answered and said, Verily I say unto you, There is <u>no man</u> that hath left house, or brethren, or sisters, or father, or mother, or wife, or children, or lands, for <u>my sake, and the gospel's.</u>" Verse 30: "But he shall receive a hundredfold now in this time, houses, and brethren, and sisters, and mothers, and children, and lands, with persecutions; and in the world to come eternal life." Verse 31: "But many that are first shall be last; and the last first."

Verse 30 is one of the scriptures that many claim for their riches and financial blessings. But, going back to verse 28, Peter states that they have given up everything to follow Jesus. However, when people read this scripture, and because Peter emphasizes that "they have given up everything to follow Jesus," the response is, "So, Lord what are we going to get out of this?" We have left our families, businesses, and friends and are now following you. All of these things are now secondary compared to our relationship with you. The apostles traveled with Jesus through Jerusalem, Judea, Samaria and Galilee. In verse 29 *Jesus answers Peter and says no man,* which included Peter, John, and James from that time until today, where we have millions and millions of those that have become saints since then. How many men? No man, none, *not a single person is left out of receiving a hundredfold of houses, lands, etc, those who have forsaken all for Jesus and the gospel's sake.*

Did Peter, John, and James actually receive a hundredfold of houses, land, etc, in their lifetime? The answer is no! What they did receive was martyrdom and imprisonment. *How many extra houses did Peter receive?* None! In fact, I believe Peter was crucified upside down. How many houses did Paul receive? None. I believe he was beheaded. Acts 12:2: King Herod killed James with the sword. Acts 7:59-60: Stephen was stoned. John died on the island of Patmos. So, the question becomes, "What have we left or forsaken to follow Jesus?" What have we given up that as we look back, it wasn't worth forsaking for the life we now and will have with Jesus? I believe we would all answer, "Nothing!" Everything we could have possibly pursued (careers, fame, money, etc.) before seeking Jesus could never have brought long-lasting purpose, peace, or hope in this life. Above all, it could have never brought eternal life!

So, what did God promise if He did not promise to make everyone rich? God promised to meet our need according to the purpose for which He called us (Phil. 4:19). He promised to equip every one of the saints to do the work for which He called us! In Romans 12:6-8, He gave gifts differently according to His grace, and one is the *gift of giving.* In Romans 12:8, the Scriptures say *He will equip some* with abundance of finances in order that they may give . . . the same as He called some to be apostles, prophets, and teachers. Not everyone is an apostle, prophet, and teacher. *Not everyone* will have the *gift of giving according to Romans 12:8.* God gives special gifts to different people. Some people are born with special talents ,such as singing. Not everyone will sing like Celine Dion. They can practice all of their lives and never sound like her.

The Christians who lived in the days of Peter, John, and James were not rewarded then, but were persecuted, slain with the sword, fed to lions, tempted, scourged, tormented, and crucified. Today some Christians leave everything to become missionaries in other countries like Afghanistan and Iraq. <u>Many have died from the time of Jesus' promise until today and *have not received* a hundredfold houses and lands.</u> Yet, Jesus said "no man." We are in the same church as Peter, John, and James, just at a later time. If in those days and since then they didn't receive a hundredfold, what makes us think that we are wiser and more blessed than Peter, James, and John?

We will all be judged at the believer's judgment seat of Christ in heaven. At that time every man will be rewarded according to his works (2 Cor. 5:10). What they did receive was death not financial prosperity. Millions of Christians, who have given up everything for Jesus, have also lost their lives. They never became rich, yet Jesus said to Peter, *"no man," not a single person* who gave up all for His sake and the gospel's would be left out of this promise. Did Jesus lie or are we the ones today who are missing it? We know Jesus never lied, so it must be *"we"* who are missing it.

What Jesus said in Matthew 19:27-30, Mark 10:28-31, and Luke 18:28-30 is just the tip of the iceberg. The promises concerning the "hundredfold" and "manifold more" are the same; it's just that each of these books of the Bible gives more detail of what Jesus said. In Romans 8:18, Paul wrote, "For I reckon that the sufferings of this present time [Peter, John, and James' time, and present day Christian times] are not worthy to be compared with the glory [God's promises] which shall be revealed in us." As related earlier, the persecution is now "today"; however, there won't be any persecution when Jesus reigns on this earth.

Let's continue on and deal with the words "now in this time" in Mark 10:30. God is a God of now. Hebrews 11:1 says, "Now faith is the substance of things hoped for, the evidence of things not seen." *The "now" in "Now faith is" refers to the spiritual realm, neither the physical nor material realm.* There is no physical evidence. Looking at another scripture, 1 John 3:2, "Beloved, <u>now</u> are we the sons of God, and it doth not yet appear what we shall be: but we know that, when he shall appear, we shall be like him; for we shall see him [Jesus] as he is." In the spiritual realm, we are the sons and daughters of God, right now, without any physical evidence. In 1John 3:2 the Bible says "It doth not yet appear" physically what we shall be. Those who have a true relationship with Jesus in the new birth (that is, they are born again) are <u>now</u> the sons and daughters of God. In Mark 10:30 is God speaking about the "now" time that we are living in today or is He speaking faith and "now" is as described in Hebrews 11:1 and 1 John 3:2? *God speaks faith; the "now" in Mark 10:30 is faith speaking.*

In other terms, God's use of the word "now" is "in this time today" or "in the earth's lifetime." The earth's lifetime is the time-frame (period) we are living in, from the promise of Jesus until the end of this earth as it is today, and is to eventually be. That is, to be eventually destroyed by fire. Mark 10:30 says ". . . and in the world [age] to come eternal life." Now wait a minute . . . "world to come." . . Once again God is speaking faith. He is speaking in the spiritual realm, because we have eternal life right now. If Jesus lives in us, we have eternal life now (spiritually); however, it does not yet appear (physically). Jesus said in John 3:16 "that whosoever believeth in him should not perish, but have everlasting life."

As Christians we have the promises of God spiritually, but some of these promises are not yet manifested. The promises of God are all true: *it is the manifestation of these promises in time or in their due season that we are missing today. It is the timing that is wrong, not the promise of financial riches that is wrong.* When Jesus came the first time, Israel missed recognizing that the Messiah had come because they looked for the restoration of Israel; it was not the full-ness of God's time. Their timing was off. Jesus came as the Lamb of God and the Jews were looking for the Lion of Judah. In the full-ness of God's time, Jesus will come again . . . this time as the King of Kings and Lord of Lords. He will come as the Lion of Judah. In Acts 1:6 the scripture reads, ". . . Lord wilt thou at this time restore again the kingdom to Israel?" The Jews at that time were looking for a physical kingdom, and Jesus said to them in verse 7, "It is not for you to know the times or the seasons, which the Father hath put in his own power." In this passage, Jesus is telling them *no, now is not the time.* Well, the news is we have been waiting for over two thousand years for Jesus to restore the kingdom to Israel.

In Romans 8:19 the apostle Paul writes, "For the earnest expectation of the creature waiteth for the manifestation of the sons of God." Even though today we are brothers and sisters in the Lord, we don't have the full manifestation of unity and love yet. This will be fully manifested at the resurrection of the saints. Neither do we have the houses and lands promised. It has not happened yet, but it will. I believe this will occur as it says in Matthew 19:28: "<u>. . . in the regeneration when the Son of man [Jesus] shall sit in the throne of his glory.</u>" These things will be manifested during the thousand-year reign of Jesus upon this earth. And in Revelation 11:15, ". . . The kingdoms of this world are [will] become the kingdoms of our Lord and of his Christ; and he shall reign for ever and ever." Jesus' administration will be in; the devil's will be out, just as one US president's administration is in and another's is out at the end of a presidential election. In Revelation 20:6, it says that we shall live and reign with Christ a thousand years.

Many, who teach that financial riches are for us today, just might be receiving their reward today. Now, it is understandable what Mark 10:31 means in regards to the promise given in Mark 10:28-31. Verse 31 says, "But many that are first . . ." Notice, the use of the word *many,* not a few, but *many* "shall be last; and the <u>last first.</u>" The first reference to "many" is in regards to those who are living today claiming and receiving their many houses and lands. The second "many" refers to those who give their all for Jesus and the gospel's sake without any material reward. <u>For example, Peter, John, James, and many other saints did not receive anything in their lifetime, but lost almost everything materially, and some even lost their lives.</u>

In Matthew 10:34-36, Jesus said that there would be division in the family because of Him. Verse 35: "For I am come to set a man at variance against his father, and the daughter against her mother . . ." Verse 36: "And a man's foes shall be they of his own household." In order to have eternal life in Christ, sometimes a person has to make a decision between Jesus and their family . . . between Jesus and the material things of this world.

We will have abundantly more than what we left in order to follow Him. In fact, there will be no comparison. The hundredfold promises that Jesus spoke about in Matthew 19:29 and Mark 10:30

were a minimum of what we are going to receive. For example, *God our heavenly Father is and will forever be more to us than all the earthly fathers* put together could ever be! *Jesus is and will be to us more than any husband, wife, child, brother, sister* could ever be and provide infinitely more than all that they could not be to us. As Jesus says in Luke 8:21, "My mother and my brethren are these which hear the word of God, and do it." Our relationship with one another will be eternally greater than any earthly relationship. *Those who hear the Word of God and do it (the true believers) will be like our spiritual mothers, brothers, sisters, wives, and husbands in Jesus.* The Scriptures say that we are a family and members of one another (1 Cor. 12). Peter has millions of spiritual mothers, brothers, and sisters. His earthly mother didn't have a hundred children, which were physical brothers and sisters. Neither did John nor James have hundreds of physical brothers and sisters, but spiritually they have millions and millions.

As Matthew 5:5 says, "Blessed are the meek: for they shall inherit the earth." Even during the one thousand-year reign of Christ, we will still be on this old earth. After the thousand years, he will create a new earth (Revelation 21:1). However, according to Matthew 19:28 (the same story as relayed in more detail in Mark 10:28-31), "And Jesus said unto them, Verily I say unto you, That ye [Peter, John, and James] which have followed me, in the regeneration . . ." When? "In the regeneration when the Son of man shall sit in the throne of his glory [during the one thousand year reign], ye [Peter, John, James, and the other apostles] also shall sit upon twelve thrones, judging the twelve tribes of Israel." *The persecution will come in today's day and the rewards, houses, lands, etc, will follow in the one thousand-year reign.* Jesus said whosoever have left father, mother (parents), wife (husband), brothers, sister, children, houses, and lands for his sake and the gospel's will receive a hundredfold now and eternal life. God will reward us for the relationships and the material things that we have left for Jesus and the gospel's sake.

We cannot just look at what is quoted in Mark 10:28-31, but must also include what is said in Matthew 19:27-31 and Luke 18:28-30 to truly understand what Jesus was saying. The regeneration of Israel has not yet occurred, but when it does (the beginning of the one thousand-year reign) at the end of the great tribulation, Jesus will reign in His glory; the twelve apostles will judge and rule Israel; and, as stated in Revelation 5:10, ". . . and we shall reign on the earth." We "who?" All the saints, not just Israel, but all those redeemed. Revelation 5:9 says, ". . . and hast redeemed us to God by thy blood out of every <u>kindred</u>, and <u>tongue</u>, and <u>people</u>, and <u>nation</u>." When Jesus reigns, there will be peace on earth. Isaiah said in Isaiah 65:25, "The wolf and the lamb shall feed together, and the lion shall eat straw like the bullock: and dust shall be serpent's meat. They shall not hurt nor destroy in all my holy mountain, saith the LORD."

So, going back to our example of the transition of one presidency to another, when Bill Clinton was president, the cabinet was Democratic. President Clinton was in power and had the authority with the Democratic cabinet to run the country. When George W. Bush became president, he replaced the Democratic cabinet with Republicans, and now he has the authority to run the country. In 2 Corinthians 4:4, *the Bible refers to Satan as "the god of this world," including the world system and the financial system.* In Ephesians 2:2, Satan is also called "the prince of the power of the air, the spirit that now worketh in the children of disobedience." I seriously doubt that out of the five hundred richest people in this world that twenty-five Christians would be among them. That's only 5 percent, indicating that the ungodly control ninety-five% or more of the world's finances. Why? Because Satan controls this world system with its greed, pride, lust, murder, terrorism, adultery, lying, and cheating spirits.

When Jesus sets up His earthly kingdom during the one thousand-year reign of Christ, then <u>we shall control everything, reigning with Christ in His glory (Revelation 5:10, 20:6).</u> *That's when the wealth of the heathen shall belong to the saints . . . it's being stored up for us now!* Matthew 5:5 says, "the meek: for they shall inherit the earth," including the manifestation of the silver and gold—that is, money. When Satan and his cabinet is thrown out of office by Jesus, then Jesus' cabinet, Israel and the saints, shall have total control in governing this earth, including financial riches.

The promise as given in Mark 10:29-30 is a spiritual promise based upon faith. The "in this time" scripture refers to the one thousand-year reign when Jesus sits upon the throne. Just as when the president, George W. Bush, came into office and brought in his cabinet to rule with him, so will it be with Jesus. We (Israel and the saints) are going to reign with Christ. Guess who will get all the benefits of Jesus' reign? As with a business you own, the company benefits would go to the employees doing the work, not to the people on the streets. And, if you owned stock in a company, you'd be the one to collect the company dividends; again, not the people on the streets. *So, we (Israel and the saints) are going to rule and reign with Him, and He is going to reward us according to our works.*

Revelation 11:15 says, "And the seventh angel sounded; and there were great voices in heaven, saying, The kingdoms of this world are become the kingdoms of our Lord, and of his Christ; and he shall reign for ever and ever." At this time, Jesus will sit on the throne of His glory in this earth. The kingdom of this world is under Satan's authority right now (2 Cor. 4:4). In Revelation 20, verse 4, John says, "I saw thrones, and they sat upon them, and judgment was given unto them . . . they lived and reigned with Christ a thousand years." Verse 5: ". . . This is the first resurrection." Verse 6: ". . . but they shall be priests of God and of Christ, and shall reign with him a thousand years." If the *apostle Paul writes to the church at Corinth that Satan is the god of this world, then he is still the god of this world.* Today, we don't have any special revelation of understanding other than what the apostles Paul, Peter, and James had. In fact, Paul wrote approximately two-thirds of the New Testament and most of what we know today comes from his writings.

When Satan tempted Jesus in the three temptations, he showed Him all the kingdoms of this world (the world system) and the glory (financial riches) of them (Matt. 4:8). Matthew 4:9: "And [Satan] saith unto him [Jesus], All these things will I give thee, if thou wilt fall down and worship me." This was a temptation, because Satan received these things (kingdoms and financial riches) from Adam. Ephesians 2:2 says, ". . . the prince of the power of the air, the spirit [Satan] that now worketh in the children of disobedience [unbelief]." Satan still controls this world system, even though Jesus defeated him at the cross. *He is not in control of us who are born again, which is the same as being saved, born of God, born of the Holy*

Spirit, born from above, born from heaven and the new birth. Don't let anyone play word games with you. If you accepted Jesus as your personal savior, according to Romans 10:9-10, *you have eternal life now* and you belong to God.

Today, we are living in what is called the church age, the time of grace. The true believers will soon be taken off this earth. 1 Corinthians 15:51 says, ". . . we shall all [believers] be changed [resurrected]." And, 1 Thessalonians 4:17, "We which are alive and remain shall be caught up [raptured] together with them [those who died in Christ] in the clouds," "so shall we ever be with the Lord." During the great tribulation, there shall be a time of great sorrow on this earth. Zechariah 14:12 speaks about a nuclear warfare occurring. "Their *flesh shall consume away while they stand* upon their feet, and their *eyes shall consume away in their holes* [eye sockets] and their *tongues shall consume away in their mouth*." Notice the words "while they stand upon their feet." They will not fall to the ground and decay. This was prophesized by Zechariah before the invention of gunpowder.

Jesus' coming with the saints will put an end to this destruction, otherwise no flesh would survive. The Antichrist and the false prophet will be cast into the lake of fire. In Revelation 20:1-3, Satan will be bound by an angel and cast into the bottomless pit for a thousand years. *Jesus will reign and the saints will possess the earth, including the financial riches (gold and silver/money)*. Jesus will put everything in order, straightening out the mess that mankind has created. Babies will still be born upon this earth. After the thousand years, Satan is going to be let loose, defeated for the last time, and cast into the lake of fire forever. In Revelation 20:11-15, the great white throne judgment will take place for all who are lost: those who rejected Jesus, including religious people who don't have a personal relationship (new birth) with Jesus.

I submit to you in this first truth that although Peter, John, and James did not receive a hundredfold houses and lands, in their time or this present age, they will be rewarded at the believers' judgment of works indicated in 2 Corinthians 5:10. At that time they will be rewarded with more than a hundredfold houses and lands during the thousand year reign of Jesus Christ upon this earth. And, so will all those today that have given up everything for Jesus and the gospel's sake. Hebrews 11:39 states, "And all these, having obtained a good testimony through faith, receive not the promise." We will not be rewarded at the judgement seat of Christ without them, the same as, "they without us should not be made perfect" (resurrected) Hebrews 11:40.

Hence, the <u>key</u> point of this truth is Matthew 19:28, "Ye which have followed me, <u>in the regeneration, when the Son of man shall sit in the throne of his glory,</u> ye also shall sit upon twelve thrones, judging the twelve tribes of Israel." Verse 29: "And everyone that has forsaken houses . . . lands for my name's sake, <u>shall receive an hundredfold</u>." Far greater than what we left for Jesus and the gospel's sake, we will have the manifestation 100 percent in us . . . the fulfillment of the fruit of the Spirit, which is love, joy, peace, longsuffering, gentleness, etc. This will be eternally greater than what our earthly family could provide for us. As far as houses and lands are concerned, Romans 8:16-17 says we are children of God, and if children then heirs of God and joint (equal) heirs with Christ. 1 Corinthians 3:21-23 says *all things (everything) are ours and* we belong to Christ and Christ is God's. Everything God has is ours!

CHAPTER 3

Truth # 2:

The New Testament (The Church Age) Scriptures Say Absolutely Nothing Positive about Financial or Material Prosperity in 3,715 Verses (97.35%) out of a Total of 3,816 Verses.

The New Testament consists of 3,816 verses starting with Acts 2:1 to Revelation 3:22 (the church age). The four Gospels, *Matthew, Mark, Luke and John,* are about the life of Jesus, *which occurs under the law of Moses (the Old Testament),* and the bringing in of the New Testament (the church age), the grace of God. When Jesus told Nicodemus that he must be born again, no one was "born again" in the four Gospels. In order for this to happen, Jesus had to die, be buried, resurrected, and *ascended on high* before He could send the Holy Ghost. This did not happen until Acts 2:1-4. Jesus told His disciples about the promise of the Father, the sending of the Holy Ghost, in the Gospel of John, chapters 14, 15, and 16; but, it was not manifested until Acts chapter 2. The new birth and the filling of the Holy Ghost were future events that were going to occur.

Jesus, Himself, lived under the law of Moses. That is why, when He healed someone, many times He told them to go show themselves to the priest *as it was commanded under the law.* In Luke 2:23, 24, when Mary brought Jesus to the temple to be presented to the Lord, she had to offer a pair of turtledoves or two young pigeons (see Lev. 12:8). *Mary lived under the law* (Gal. 4:4); and Jesus lived under the law. Jesus came to fulfill the law. He fulfilled the law in order to redeem all who were under the law.

Of the 3,816 verses in Acts 2:1 to Revelation 3:22, *only 101* say something about financial or material prosperity in a positive manner. There are *40 verses* that speak negatively about financial or material prosperity in the New Testament (church age). Most ministers who preach on financial prosperity say very little or nothing at all about these 40 negative verses. Percentage-wise, the 101 positive verses on financial or material prosperity represent 2.65 percent of the New Testament. The remaining 3,715 verses, 97.35 percent, say absolutely nothing or something negative about financial or material prosperity. Following this percentage formula in relation to what I teach about on Sundays in terms of financial (money) and material things would represent one Sunday and 22 minutes of the next Sunday. This is based on teaching 52 one hour sermons per year. I would not be able to say one word about money or material things the other 50 Sundays and 38 minutes in the year. Is that what we hear today? No, what we hear is a lot of preaching on money, money, money, and more money! I once heard a preacher say, "What we really need is *more* money to get the gospel out."

No, what we really need is a greater manifestation of the Holy Spirit! We need to be more obedient and live a lifestyle of holiness. God will provide the money if we seek His face and not so much His hand. Preaching a lot about money *is not* New Testament Bible. Again, I reiterate, 97.35 percent of the New Testament verses say nothing about money or material things. We are not bound by a percentage formula; however, it gives us something to think about. If, being millionaires, having a lot of money was so important in the eyes of God, why isn't this subject included in the New Testament as much as it is preached today? This kind of preaching is totally out of proportion with the New Testament Scriptures.

Let's look at each book in the New Testament. There are a total of 23 books from Acts 2:1 to Revelation 3:22 (church age). There are 3,816 verses in these 23 books, of which only 101 speak positively about finances and material things. These 101 verses include those Scriptures that speak definitively about the subject and those that hint toward finances and material things in a positive manner. I put these in the category of a "gray area." There were approximately ten verses that fit this category. For example, if the verse said that God blessed us *in everything,* I include it in the 101 verses.

There are *10 books of the 23 books in the New Testament that do not have one verse or word about financial or material things.* These are Ephesians, 155 total verses—0 on financial or material things; Colossians, 95 verses—0 on financial or material things; 1 Thessalonians, 89 verses—0 on financial or material things; 2 Thessalonians, 47 verses, 0 verses; 2 Timothy, 83 verses, 0 verses; Titus, 46 verses, 0 verses; 1 Peter, 105 verses, 0 verses; 2 John, 13 verses, 0 verses; Jude, 25 verses, 0 verses; and Revelation, 71 verses, 0 verses. These ten books, which don't say a single positive word on financial or material things, do, however, contain some negative verses. An example is 1 Peter 1:18, which says, ". . . not redeemed with *corruptible* things as silver and gold [money] . . ."

Additionally, there are *three other books* where I found only *1 verse* on financial or material things. These are in Galatians, a total of 149 verses, 1 verse (6:6) on financial prosperity; 2 Peter, 61 verses, 1 verse (1:3); and 3 John, 14 verses, 1 verse (2). There is *one book,* Philemon, which has a total of 25 verses, that *contains 1-½ verses* (18, 19) on financial or material things. When a verse speaks both positively and negatively, I credit it as a half verse. Philemon 18 says, "If he wronged thee, or oweth [negative] thee ought, put that on mine account [positive]."

Continuing on with the list of books that contain verses on financial or material things, there is *one,* the book of James, which contains *2 verses* (2:16; 5:7) out of a total of 108 verses. There is *one book,* 1 John, out of 105 verses, contains *3 ½ verses* (3:22; 5:14, 15; 3:17). There is *one book,* the book of Romans, which contains *5 verses* (13:6, 7; 15:26, 27, 28) out of a total of 433 verses. There is *Philippians,* with a total of 104 verses containing *6 verses (*)* on financial /material things. There is *one book,* 1 Timothy, out of 111 verses, contains *7 verses (*);* the *book of Hebrews,* out of 302 verses, contains *9 verses (*); 1 Corinthians,* out of 437 verses, *14 verses (*);* the *book of Acts,* out of 981 verses contains *23 verses (*);*

and finally, *one book,* 2 Corinthians, <u>*27 verses (*)*</u> out of a total of 257 verses. Altogether, there are 17 books with 5 verses or less (10 with none) and only 6 books with 7 verses or more that speak about financial or material things.

There are many surprises when you dig into the Scriptures. One thing to my surprise and shock was that out of the 3, 816 Scriptures in the <u>New Testament,</u> the word <u>"money" was mentioned only seven times.</u> Of the seven times, *five times in a negative way, only one time in a positive way (Acts 4:37),* and one time what I would call neither positive nor negative, but more of a tie. This one scripture, which I consider a tie, is a quote from the Old Testament mentioned in the book of Hebrews. I call it a tie because the writer of Hebrews is talking about the word money in both a positive and negative manner. Remembering that the <u>four Gospels took place under the Old Testament,</u> where the word *"money"* is mentioned over 100 times (*see Truth #3*).

Now, the word <u>"rich,"</u> which I deal with in Truth #4, has *only one positive verse* out of the total 3,816 verses. When God showed this to me I said, "God are you serious, I know you have a sense of humor, I mean come on Lord?" The word <u>"prosperity"</u> *is not in the New Testament!* This word appears *absolutely zero times* in the New Testament. This was the second thing that shocked me. The third shock was that the word <u>"prosper"</u> is mentioned <u>*only in one verse,*</u> 3 John 2. Jesus says, out of the mouth of two or three witnesses, let every word be established. Here, we have the word "prosper" mentioned only once, not two or three times!

Now, let's look at the book of Philippians, it has 104 verses with 6 verses that are positive regarding finances. They are all in Chapter 4 verses 10, 15, 16, 17, 18 and 19. When we give our finances to God first, He tells us that our giving is a sweet smell in His nostrils. Second, it is a sacrifice acceptable and third, it is well pleasing to Him (verse 18). In verse 19, Paul writes, "But my God shall supply all your need, according to his riches in glory by Christ Jesus." <u>He did not say He was going to make us rich or that we would become millionaires.</u> No! This means He is going to help us pay our bills, our rent or mortgage, our car note, etc. on or before the due date because at that moment that is what *our need is.* If our finances are messed up, don't blame God! He will help us and keep us from being overcome with debt if we are reasonable in taking care of our finances. We are diligent in business, working and not overspending nor sitting at home not wanting to work.

He promises to help us and bless us if we seek first His Kingdom and His righteousness (Matthew 6:33). We don't need to seek things. God knows our name and where we live. In Hebrews 1:2, it says, "(God) hath in these last days spoken unto us by his Son, whom he hath appointed heir of all things." Romans 8:17 says, we are joint heirs with Christ. The "all things" I added into the 101 verses identified as speaking positive about finances because all things would include finances.

Seven verses (2, 3, 4, 5, 6, 8 and 9) in Hebrews Chapter 7 speak about finances; however, these are *verses out of the Old Testament* that are being quoted by the writer of Hebrews. Hebrews 7:5 tells us that the Levites were "commanded" to take tithes from the people according to the law of Moses. We are not under the law of Moses, but, under the New Testament (grace). Abraham paid tithes to God through Melchizedek, the King of Salem and priest of God, out of his love for God. It was not because he was commanded to pay tithes. Melchizedek was a type of Jesus (verse 3). Abraham paid tithes to God because of his love for God and *so should we pay tithes and offerings to God because we love him (Truth #12).* We are not commanded in the New Testament, Church Age, to pay tithes. "And here men" (Levites on earth) "that die receive tithes, but there he" (Jesus) "receiveth them of whom it is witnessed that he liveth." But, there…where is there? But there in heaven Jesus receives our tithes because it is witnessed that Jesus lives. So, when you give your tithes you are giving them to Jesus from your heart out of love. Jesus receives your tithes in heaven so that His work can be done on this earth. Verse 8 is the only verse of the 3,816 verses of the New Testament that refers to New Testament tithing.

I believe the odds of me missing or erring in these 3,816 verses are 1/10 of 1 percent; this is less than 4 verses. Ten percent of 3,816 would be 382 verses and 1 percent would be 38 verses. So, 1/10 of 1 percent is 3.8; this is less than 4 verses. I don't believe the error margin is more than 4 verses for miscounting the New Testament, church age, verses from Acts 2:1 to Revelation 3:22.

If I were talking to someone about Jesus 97.35 percent of the time, they would say He is a person who must love Jesus. But, if I were talking to them *about money the same 97.35% of the time, they would say he must love money and has itching ears* when it comes to money. So, we can see how today preaching on financial prosperity is blown way out of proportion. This is causing people to have itching ears (2 Timothy 4:3). *Jesus said, "Out of the abundance of the heart the mouth speaketh" (Matt. 12:34).* We talk most about what is important and dear to us. Hence, we should talk (and teach) more about loving God, loving one another, and living a life of obedience and holiness. I mean <u>really</u> loving one another as God commanded us, not what we call love today in most churches.

Therefore, I submit to you the <u>key</u> point of Truth # 2 is if financial riches were so important to God for us today, <u>why wasn't it written all over the New Testament as in the Old Testament</u> (Genesis 1:1 through Acts 1:26), which is full of financial and material prosperity?

* See Index for scripture verses.

CHAPTER 4

Truth # 3:

The Old Testament Was a Shadow, Type, Copy, Figure, Pattern, or Example of the Truth to Come That Jesus Fulfilled in the New Testament

Truth # 3 is probably the most difficult for some to accept and understand. All of the spiritual things are true because God's Word does not change spiritually. Most of the material and physical things of the Old Testament were a shadow, type, copy, figure, pattern, or examples of the truth to come that Jesus fulfilled in the New Testament (Heb. 8:5; 9:9,23,24; 10:1; Col. 2:16,17). Some might say that was only under the law of Moses.

So, I will start before the law of Moses during the time of Adam and Eve. Abel slew an animal and he offered it to God. He also built an altar out of rocks and worshipped God. Do we build altars today out of rocks and worship God with animal sacrifices? NO! John 4:24: "God is a Spirit and they that worship him must worship him in spirit and in truth." We worship God spiritually; we don't need material or physical sites anymore to worship God truly. We assemble in a building; it is not the church. We, God's people, are the church; we are the spiritual body of Christ. Many people, denominational and nondenominational, pass in front a church building, and they will say, "That's the church." They will tell you not to smoke or speak evil in the church. Then they will go outside to smoke three cigarettes, or curse, or gossip about someone.

Wait a minute: we are the church. Jesus didn't die for a building; He died for us! Jesus told the woman at the well in John 4:21, "the hour cometh when you shall neither, in this mountain nor yet at Jerusalem, worship the Father." Today, true worship has nothing to do with material things, either financial or physical. In the Old Testament, the material and physical things were a shadow, type, example, or copy of the truth to come. Truth # 3 is that God blessed His people Israel under the *Old Testament with material and financial things because no one was born again*. Today, under the *New Testament, the true riches are the spiritual riches because we are born again and we have eternal life*. Jesus says in John 4:23, "But the hour cometh, and now is . . ." He is speaking faith as the Holy Spirit had not yet come, because Jesus was not yet been glorified.

You must be born again, with the Holy Spirit living within your spirit, in order for you to worship God truly. No one was born again until Acts 2:1-4, the coming of the Holy Spirit, the promise of the Father. Today, people want to go to Jerusalem and be baptized in the Jordan River so they can feel closer to God. God is in you and with you if you are a true child of God; you can worship God right now where you are. You don't need an altar like Abraham or to go to Jerusalem to worship God. Did you read what Jesus said in John 4:21, "neither in this mountain, nor yet at Jerusalem, worship the Father?"

The Old Testament was full of material and physical things so that Israel could approach God. Most people always want to see something before they believe. You can worship God while walking down the street, by saying, "I worship You, Lord, thank You, Jesus, and I love You, Lord," as long as it's coming from your heart. That would be truly worshipping God, and it has nothing to do with material or physical things.

In the Old Testament, the Promised Land was the land of Canaan (Israel), a land filled with milk and honey, an abundance of material and physical things. *God blessed them with financial, material, and physical things in abundance because no one was born again, that was their Promised Land.* <u>What is the Promised Land today?</u> <u>The kingdom of God spiritually;</u> it's not the land of Canaan anymore. Abraham had a revelation of today's Promised Land in Hebrews 11:10, 16. The Promised Land to Israel was physically the land of Canaan, and He dealt with them outwardly because no one was born again.

God led them by a cloud in the day and by a fire at night. Do we think God will lead us by a cloud by day and by a fire by night? No! These were figures of the Spirit of God that was to come to guide and lead us in all truth. God leads us by His Spirit, by a still small voice, or He will lead us through His Word. The Spirit of God will speak to us spiritually within our spirit. Hebrew 11:8: "By faith Abraham, when he was called to go out into a place which he should after receive for an inheritance, he obeyed God . . ." Abraham was given the land of Canaan (physical) and *God gave it to him because no one was born again.* That's not what Abraham was looking for; he was looking for an eternal city. He went out not knowing where he was going, and by faith (trusting in God) he sojourned in the land of promise. In other words, he went to Canaan, but that's all he could receive. It had to be something physical or material because *everyone was spiritually dead, separated from God because of sin.* Abraham looked for a city that had a foundation, whose builder and maker is God (not man).

In the land of Canaan, they conquered and possessed the cities (manmade), which is what Israel received, but that's not what Abraham was looking for. Abraham was way ahead of everyone else. He was living under the Old Testament, but he had a vision by faith of the New Testament, the New Jerusalem that God has prepared for us today. We haven't received it yet, and we won't until God creates the new heaven and new earth after the thousand-year reign. Hebrews 11:10: "For <u>he looked for a city</u> which hath foundations, <u>whose builder and maker is God.</u>"

Hebrews 11:12: "Therefore, sprang there even of one [Abraham] and him as good as dead [because he's around one hundred years old now], so many as the stars of the sky [That's all his of descendants, which is all of us; spiritual not the physical stars. You cannot count the physical stars of the sky or the descendants of Abraham] in multitude, and as the sand which is by the sea shore innumerable [uncountable]." Verse 13: "These [Abraham included] all died in faith, not having received the promises. [He didn't see his descendants physically who inherited the Kingdom of God.] *But having seen them afar off,* and were persuaded of them, and embraced them, and *confessed that they were strangers and pilgrims on the earth."*

We are the children of Abraham (spiritually); we are strangers on the what? The earth that Satan controls today as the god of this world (2 Cor. 4:4) is how we should see it. We should not be seeking things, or to become millionaires. If we seek God, He will meet our need. Don't misunderstand me: God doesn't want us broke; He wants to meet our need (Phil. 4:19). Jesus said in Matthew 6:32 that our heavenly Father knows that we have <u>need of the things</u> which the Gentiles seek after, but many Christians are seeking these things. Someone might say we are not seeking financial riches.

Jesus said, "For out of the abundance of the heart the mouth speaks" (Matt. 12:34). <u>If you are constantly speaking or preaching about financial prosperity, Jesus says this is what is in your heart.</u> Do we believe Jesus or man? Jesus! Case closed. Hebrews 11:14: "For they that say such things declare plainly that they seek a country." Verse 15: "And truly if they had been mindful of that country [Egypt] from which they came out . . ." Verse 16: "But now they desire a better country, that is, an heavenly, wherefore God is not ashamed to be called their God: for he hath prepared for them a city."

"A HEAVENLY CITY, A HEAVENLY COUNTRY"—that's what Abraham was looking for; he was not looking for an earthly country. He was looking for a heavenly Jerusalem; Abraham was not looking for a physical or a material city or country (Canaan), but that was all he could receive under the Old Testament, which was an example of what was to come. Jesus had not yet been glorified. God gave to Abraham and his descendants the land of Canaan. Abraham was looking for a heavenly country; he wasn't looking for an earthly country, but God couldn't give it to him then. *Today, we are doing the opposite of what we should be doing.* <u>We are under the new covenant and in the spiritual blessing of God, yet many are focusing on material things.</u>

There was the temple of God (material) that Solomon built. It was destroyed, and then Zerubbabel rebuilt it and Herod enlarged it. Today, who's the temple of God? We are the temple of God (spiritually)! Know ye not that your body is the temple of God; the Spirit of God dwells in our spirit, which dwells in our body (1 Cor. 6:19). When we die and they put our bodies in the grave, the Holy Spirit is not in the grave. The Holy Spirit lives in our spirit, which goes into the presence of God. We have the Spirit of the Lord in us; we drink of the Spirit, He's in our spirit, which is in our body. <u>1 Corinthians 12:13 says we are baptized into one body (the true church, it is spiritual, Col. 1:18) by the Spirit of God</u>; it's a spiritual birth.

The *physical temple* of the Old Testament used to be the house of God. God's presence was there in a sense that this is where He spoke to them, or in *the tabernacle of Moses,* where God came down to speak to Israel. Today, people make a big deal out of things: like searching for the ark of the covenant, Noah's ark, or the robe that Jesus wore. We don't need any of these things; all we need is faith in God's Word! God lives in us (true believers) by His Spirit; God's glory is in us. "Christ in us the hope of glory" (Col. 1:27). All these physical and material things, as the glory of the ark of the covenant, were done away within Jesus. They were types and shadows of things to come.

Here are some more examples in the Old Testament: Passover used to be celebrated with the blood of animals, goats and sheep. We don't have to observe Passover anymore. God sees the blood of Jesus (spiritual), and not the blood of animals (physical). Where's the blood of animals? It's on this earth. Where's the blood of Jesus? It's in heaven. John the Baptist said, "Behold the Lamb of God," because Jesus was to be offered as a lamb sacrifice. The old covenant had rams, lambs, and goats that Israel offered up with their blood for a sacrifice.

Under the New Testament (spiritual), it's the blood of Jesus. Let's look at another one: 2 Corinthians 3:3: God's Word was written on tables of stone, the Ten Commandments, the law of Moses. Where is God's Word written now? It is written in our hearts. A person can destroy the paper of the Bible: mine is all scribble, torn, and falling apart. Before I became born again, I had a Bible, which I never used, and I kept it all nice and neat. This is not what God wants; *He wanted His Word in us, written in our hearts, and in our spirit.*

The Old Testament material and physical things were a type, a shadow, an image, or an example of spiritual things to come, which are infinitely greater. Today, we have the real thing. The Old Testament was pointing to the New Testament, and the reality of God's presence that would be in us. 2 Corinthians 3:3: "Forasmuch as ye are manifestly [made known] declared to the epistle [the letters], of Christ ministered by us, written <u>not with ink, but with the Spirit of the living God [the Spirit of God lives in us]; *not in tables of stone . . ."*</u> like those Moses received at Mount Sinai. The Bible says His word is written "in fleshy tables of the heart" inside our body right now.

When we speak God's Word, we are speaking to the person's spiritual heart. God gave me the revelation of what I'm writing; it is God's grace! I believe there are millions of others who have this same revelation. It's not of me but of God, because I was trying to get away from teaching this. Paul says he was pressed in the spirit; so was I. God is sovereign. He doesn't need a fifty thousand-member church or a ten thousand-member church, and there is nothing wrong with the size of these churches. God does as He wills.

We have gone to itching ears, going astray, and seeking materialistic and financial things just like the world. We have gone back to the Old Testament, to the money and riches of Solomon. "I'll give you a new heart," He said, "and I'm going to write these things in your spirit (spiritual) and *not on table of stones (material)."* In John 6:27, Jesus tells the people not to labor (work, seek, go after) meat (food, physical, material), which perishes, but for that which endures unto everlasting life (spiritual) that the Son of Man shall give unto you. In John 6:31, God gave them physical manna from heaven, right?

Jesus said in verse 35, "I am the true bread from heaven [spiritual]." The people said that Moses gave them true bread, physical manna, but Jesus said, "No! I am the true bread from heaven [spiritual]." Let's look at some more examples and shadows by going to Hebrews 8:6: "but now hath <u>he obtained a more excellent ministry, by how much also he is the mediator of a better covenant, which</u>

was established upon better promises." *We have a better covenant than the Old Testament. I just want you to remember that the New Testament is better than the Old, which is full of shadows, copies, examples, and figures.*

Hebrews 10:19 says we can "enter into the holiest by the blood of Jesus [spiritual]," where under the Old Testament, only the high priest could go. The high priest was a man, a descendent of Aaron, Moses' brother (physical). Hebrews 8:1 says that Jesus is our high priest (spiritual). We can enter spiritually into the holy of holies because we are born of God, the Holy Ghost signifying that the way into the holiest of all was not yet manifested while the first tabernacle was yet standing, which was *a figure for the time then present*. God sees us enter into the holy of holies in the spirit. We cannot see this until we shed our bodies, and then we will see clearly as God see us.

These material and financial things were figures. Now you say, "What about the spiritual things?" The spiritual things are eternal; for example, in the song "Praise the Lord," you can praise Him today and forever. The earth and the fullness thereof belong to the Lord. The silver and gold belong to God, because *everything* belongs to the Lord! The universe belongs to the Lord; however, there's a time and a season, beginning with the thousand-year reign, where we will posses all these material and financial things, not today. You see all these things are just a figure or type in the Old Testament. Hebrews 9:9: "Which was a *figure for the time then present,* in which were offered both gifts and sacrifices, that could not make him that did the service perfect, as pertaining to the conscience." It couldn't make us perfect, but we know the blood has made us perfect in Him.

The Old Testament tabernacle was a figure for that time where they offered sacrifices which couldn't make man perfect, which stood only in meats and drinks, diver washings and fleshly command-ments (ordinances) imposed on them until the time of reformation. *All these shadows, figures, types, and examples were until Jesus.* Verse 11: ". . . an high priest of good things to come . . ." In the Old Testament, all those things pointed to Jesus. Verse 21: "Moreover he sprinkled with blood both the tabernacle, and all the vessels of the ministry." Verse 22: "And almost all things are by the law purged with blood; and without shedding of blood is no remission." Verse

23: "It was therefore necessary that the *patterns* of the things in the heavens . . ." The *patterns* were symbolic representations of the New Testament things; they were material, physical, and financial. The gold and the silver symbolize the true riches of God's kingdom, eternal life and spiritual riches—love, grace, mercy, longsuffering, faith, and good works. Remember in the Old Testament everyone was spiritually poor; no one had eternal life.

The blood of Jesus, which is in heaven, purifies the heavenly things and us. We are not purified with the blood of animals (physical). The heavenly things themselves should be purified with better sacrifices than these. Verse 24: "For Christ is not entered into the holy places made with hands [material], which are *figures of the true;* but into heaven itself [spiritual] . . ." That is where Jesus is now—to appear in the presence of God for us. All the teachings about giving money, saying that we had better give so that you can receive the riches of this earth, are not New Testament teaching. The motive of our giving of tithes and offerings should be based on our love for Him and people. We give to God because we love the Lord; He first loved us, and not because He is going to make us a millionaire or make us rich. God never promised to make us rich or a millionaire.

God promised to supply all of our needs (Phil. 4:19). Hebrews 10:1: "For the law of Moses having *a shadow* . . . [that's all it was] . . . of good things to come . . ." Romans 6: 14 says that we are not under the law of Moses anymore but under grace. The law was a shadow of faith to draw us to Christ so that we could have faith in him. A shadow is something that passes away, it is not the real thing; it points us to the real thing. Somebody sees our shadow and they say "oh there's your shadow." That's the shadow of us; we are the real person, not the shadow. *These material things were shadows, examples, copies, and figures of better things to come.*

Hebrews 10:1 says the law was a *shadow* of good things to come (spiritual), but they could never with those sacrifices that they offered year-by-year make themselves perfect. Jesus made us perfect by what He has done for us and not by what we do. Thank God! Hebrews 11:17: "By faith Abraham, when he was tried, he offered up Isaac: and he that had received the promises [Abraham] offered up his only begotten son," his only born son. Verse 18: "Of whom it was said that in Isaac [God had made a promise] shall thy seed be called." Now wait a minute: Isaac does not have any children, but Abraham was going to kill him upon the altar. Verse 19: Abraham was accounting that God was able to raise Isaac up from the dead from whence also he received him as *a figure.* Isaac was just a figure of Jesus spiritually, Jesus was born of the Holy Spirit, and He's the Son of God. He's perfect! Jesus is God in the flesh that came down to this earth. Isaac was just a figure, in other words he was a fore-runner, a copy of the truth. Jesus was the one who was going to be raised from the dead, but Abraham believed that God was going to raise Isaac from the dead, that's the kind of faith Abraham had. This man's faith was so great that he believed God was going to raise Isaac from the dead because he had a promise from God; it was neither about money nor material things.

In Colossians 2:14, the work of Jesus is described as "Blotting out of the handwriting of ordinances that was against us, which was contrary to us and took it out of the way, nailing it to the cross." In other words, at the cross Jesus took all these things that was contrary to us away. Verse 15: "And having spoiled principalities and powers [demonic spirits], he made a show of them openly, triumphing over the in it [the cross]." Verse 16: "Let no man therefore judge you in meat, or in drink, or in respect of a holyday or the new moon, or of the sabbath days." Verse 17: "Which are *a shadow of things to come;* but the body of Christ." Jesus is alive, there's no more focusing on these *shadows, they are done away within Him!* Verse 18: "Let no man beguile you [in other words let no man cheat you] of your reward in a voluntary humility and worshipping of angels or intruding into those things . . ."which was just a shadow. Don't let anybody cheat you.

Chapter 5 of Romans, verse 13: "For until the law [the law of Moses] sin was in the world: but sin is not imputed sin when there is no law." Before Moses gave the law, God did not impute sin on the people as like under the law. Once the law came, then they were conscious of breaking the law. Romans 5:14: "Nevertheless death reigned from Adam to Moses [even before the law people still died], even over them that had not sinned after the similitude of Adam's transgression . . ." The first Adam willfully rejected the Word of God and listened to the devil; he was tempted and he was disobedient in the Garden of Eden; nevertheless death still reigned because the people had a sin nature born of Adam, who was a contrasting type of Christ. Jesus is the last Adam who gives us spiritual life.

Here are some other examples of the Old Testament material things that Jesus fulfilled in the New Testament spiritually. Egypt was a type of the world and God's people Israel were kept in bondage under Pharaoh (physically). Pharaoh was a type of Satan who had us in the bondage of sin. However, Jesus freed us from the bondage of Satan's sin. Moses also was a type of Jesus, he freed Israel from Pharaoh. In the Old Testament we have Egypt (the world), Pharaoh (Satan), and physical bondage (sin). Moses was Israel's savior, sent by God to *deliver them physically.*

In the New Testament, Jesus is the Savior who God sent to deliver us from the *bondage of sin spiritually.* In the Old Testament, Israel went out to battle against the Philistines, the Amalekites, and the Babylonians (physical). The New Testament tells us we wrestle not against flesh and blood, but against principalities and the powers of darkness (spiritual).

In the Old Testament, people burnt (physical) incense with their prayers. In the New Testament, we don't need to burn incense. The Spirit of God sanctifies our prayers (Rom. 15:16, spiritual). In the Old Testament, Israel (God's people) was commanded to keep the Passover, the Sabbaths, and other holy days, as shown in Leviticus 23 (physical). Today, we are not bound by certain days or feast days because Christ is our Passover and He fulfilled all these things for us (1 Cor. 5:7). Romans 14:5-9 says every day, including our whole lives, belongs to the Lord. You can celebrate any day that you desire in the Lord, but you are not commanded to do so. Jesus fulfilled all the Old Testament at the cross.

In certain churches, if the members don't show up for Easter Sunday services (what we call Resurrection Sunday), then they are told that they have committed a major sin. Romans 14:6: "He that regardeth the day, regardeth it unto the Lord, and he that regardeth not the day, to the Lord he doth not regard it." In the Old Testament, circumcision was of the flesh (physical); however, in the •New

Testament according to Romans 2:29, circumcision is of the heart (spiritual) and not of the flesh.

The <u>key</u> point is there are many examples, shadows, copies, types, patterns, and figures in the Old Testament that Jesus fulfilled for us. <u>All of these are done away with in Christ Jesus, and to hold on to these material and financial things is</u> *<u>to dishonor His redemptive work.</u>* *This is very important because we are taking away from His glory.* <u>He did it all; it is finished!</u> <u>Case closed.</u>

Under the Old Testament, no one was born again; they were all spiritually dead, so God's "Promised Land" and blessings to Israel were financial, physical, and material. *That's all they could receive under the Old Testament.*

Under the New Testament, God's "Promised Land" and true blessings are spiritual (Kingdom of God) because of Jesus Christ. We are born again and have eternal life with the Spirit of God living in us, which Israel could not receive under the Old Testament. In Truth # 11, I will prove to you that the blessing of Abraham (the promise of the Spirit, Gal. 3:14) was that the Spirit of God would live in us. It was not about us receiving an abundance of riches and money. This is God's great and glorious promise to Abraham.

CHAPTER 5

Truth # 4:

Out of All the Teachings We Hear About the Word "Prosper," 3 John 2 is the Only Verse in the New Testament Where It Appears

In 3 John 2, it says, "Beloved I wish above all things that thou mayest prosper and be in health, even as thy soul prospereth." This verse says nothing about money, but if we give it the benefit of the doubt and say it is referring to money, then what we are saying is that this reference to money appears only one time in the New Testament. In a <u>single verse out of 3,816 verses, the word "prosper" appears.</u> Some say this passage is referring to financial prosperity, which it does not really say; but I am allowing the benefit of the doubt. However, this is the *only time the word "prosper" appears in the entire New Testament*. How do we wind up making a doctrine out of that?

From the Old Testament, I showed in Truth # 3 that the reference to the word "prosper" referred to blessings that were material. *Forty-eight times the word "prosper" (materially) appears in the Old Testament*. God dealt with Israel under the Old Testament in abundance with material things because they were spiritually dead. He could not give them spiritual things because Jesus had not yet come. When Jesus did come into the world, God was able to deal with us spiritually; hence, in the New Testament He does. For example, like the new birth, we are born of God; we are sons and daughters of God and not just servants of God. *Prior to Jesus, no one was born again,* but their faith was counted unto them for righteousness.

It is like having a check. You cannot cash a check anywhere. You cash the check where people know you. For instance, if you live in the United States and go to Mexico and try to cash a check, it would be very difficult if at all possible; they most likely wouldn't cash it. But if you gave them US dollar bills, the real thing, they would take it. Go to China; although it is illegal for the common people to have cash money, they would take the money. Try to cash a check in China and see if they would accept it. No. A check is only a shadow of the true money. Hence, in the Old Testament, the material and financial blessings God gave Israel were only a shadow of the spiritual blessings to come.

The word "prospered" appears *one time in the New Testament*. In this instance, 1 Corinthians 16:2, God is speaking about money. This scripture says, Let everyone as he has prospered lay aside money on the first day of the week to give when Paul arrives. One time this word appears in the New Testament; however, it appears *twelve times* in *the Old Testament*. When you combine these two words "prosper" and "prospered," they appear in the New Testament *only two times;* once in 3 John 2, where we are giving them the benefit of the doubt and allowing a financial meaning, and in 1 Corinthians 16:2. In the Old Testament, both words appeared a total of *sixty times*. How are we going to justify this before God?

The word "prospereth" appears in the New Testament only *one time,* and it appears *three times* in the Old Testament. That one time appearance in the New Testament is a spiritual reference. In 3 John 2, it says, "Beloved I wish above all things that you may prosper and be in health, even as your soul prospereth." Your soul is not your spirit or body. Your soul is your awareness of life, your five senses, your will, and your emotions. This awareness occurs in the spiritual realm. Thus, we have the words "prosper," "prospered," and "prospereth" appearing *two times financially* (materially) and *one time spiritually* in the New Testament. The words "prosper," "prospered," and "prospereth" appear in the Old Testament for a total of *sixty-three times*.

Let's now look at the words "prosperity," "prosperous," and "prosperously." The word "prosperity" appears *zero times* in the New Testament. Out of 3,816 verses in the New Testament, not a single time is the word "prosperity" mentioned. It is mentioned in the Old Testament *seventeen times*. The word "prosperous" is mentioned *once* in the New Testament, and it is mentioned *seven times* in the Old Testament. The one time in the New Testament is Romans 1:10, which states that Paul might have a prosperous (successful) journey. That does not mean that he was going to make a lot of money and become rich. It meant he was going to have a successful journey, that everything would be okay. The word "prosperously" is mentioned *zero times* in the New Testament, and *two times* in the Old Testament.

In all the New Testament, these words—prosper, prospered, prospereth, prosperity, prosperous, and prosperously—are mentioned for a total of *only four* times, twice materially and twice spiritually. A prosperous (successful) journey is spiritual. The other reference is "even as your soul prospereth," which is spiritual. These words are *mentioned eighty-nine times* in the Old Testament.

There are only two verses in the Old Testament about Jabez (1 Chron. 4:9-10), and yet people have written books about Jabez's financial prosperity. Why do we have to think it was about money? How do we know he was not speaking about enlarging his spiritual borders? How do we know? Were we there? No. We are being presumptuous. That is all there is on Jabez in the Bible, two verses. He asked the Lord to enlarge his borders, and we presume that it was material or financial. Anything to prove that prosperity means money. Even if he was asking for material blessings, that's all he could receive. He could not ask God for eternal life or to receive the Holy Spirit because Jesus hadn't come.

We took these two verses and wrote many books. This is called presumption. We are presuming that financial prosperity is what Jabez was speaking about. He might have been saying, "Lord, enlarge my borders of my godly influence in other people's lives." Since he was speaking to God and *many people did not know God at that time,* his request could have been for God to allow him to influence them to follow Him. How did we know he was not speaking about that? It is presumptuous. Even if it was materially, it is in the Old Testament.

Galatians 4:4: "But when the fulness of the time was come [that is <u>God's time, not ours</u>], <u>God sent forth his son Jesus</u> made of a woman, <u>made under the law</u>." Mary lived under the law of Moses, and so did Jesus. What did Jesus come to do? He came to redeem those under the law. He redeemed us by His blood. He came to redeem all of the people that were under the law, Israel and the sinners (world — 1 Tim. 1:9).

The four books of the Gospel, as pointed out in Truth # 3, are placed in the New Testament, but they actually occurred under the Old Testament. As indicated above, *Jesus' life took place under the law of Moses.* Although Jesus spoke about the new birth, no one was born again until Acts 2:1. In John's Gospel, He spoke about the promise of the Father, the coming of the Holy Ghost. In fact, the promise to Abraham was not a promise that we were going to receive a lot of money, such as the financial riches of Abraham. <u>The promise was that we were going to receive the Spirit of God</u> — <u>who would abide in us</u>. Paul said, "The promise of the Spirit" —that means we have the Spirit of God in us. Not "promises" of the Holy Spirit, which would include having a bunch of things. NO! The promise is that the Holy Spirit is going to live in us. Many have the promise of Abraham all wrong. Remember Galatians 4:4 says Jesus was sent forth to redeem those that were under the law. Revelations 5:9 says, "And they sung a new song saying, Thou art worthy to take the book, and to open the seals thereof: for thou wast slain and hast redeemed us to God by thy blood."

Jesus lived under the law, the Old Testament, which includes the four Gospels, even though they are listed in the New Testament. However, it does not stop there, because Paul said in 1 Corinthians 15:17 without the resurrection of Jesus, we are yet dead in our sins. It is the resurrection of Jesus that gives us new life. The death of Jesus remits our sins, but it is the resurrection that gives us eternal life. So now you see, the Gospels were under the law; Jesus lived under the law, because He Himself had not yet been resurrected.

That is why He said all righteousness, to John the Baptist, must be fulfilled. Read Luke 2:22-24 where Mary had to present Jesus to the Lord in Jerusalem, according to the days of her purification, and she had to offer up a sacrifice to the Lord, which *they were commanded to do under the law* (Lev. 12:4-8).

Let's now look at the word "<u>money</u>" as it actually appears in the Bible. This one blew me away. In the Old Testament, the word "money" is mentioned *115 times,* and in the four Gospels (Matthew, Mark, Luke, and John), *16 times*, for a total of *131 times*. It is mentioned in the New Testament *7 times—1 time* in a positive way, *5 times* negatively, and *1 time* as a quote from the Old Testament. When we read the Bible, is it different than what we are hearing on TV? <u>Is God warning us about today's teachings on money?</u> For the love of money is the root of all evil. Go buy a *Strong's Exhaustive Concordance* and see if what I am writing is true or not. Do not believe what people are saying when it is different from what is written in the Bible.

In the <u>Old Testament,</u> the word "<u>rich</u>" is mentioned twice spiritually, *one time* in Zechariah 11:5, and *one time* in Luke 12:21. Remember, God blessed His people in the Old Testament with material and financial blessings in abundance. In the New Testament, Acts 2:1 thru Revelation 3:22, the word "rich" (materially) is mentioned *seven times, all negatively.* In the New Testament, the word "rich" (spiritually) is spoken of *positively nine times,* none negatively. Even though I've previously stated that the four Gospels are under the Old Testament, I will separate them from the Old Testament in the following writings.

<u>Materially and financially</u>, the words "rich," "riches," "richer," "richly," "enrich," "enriched," "enriches," "wealth," and "wealthy" are mentioned in the Old Testament. <u>"Rich"</u> (materially) is mentioned *thirty-one times* in the Old Testament and *sixteen times* in the Gospels, for a total of *forty-seven times* (materially). It is mentioned *only twice (spiritually)* in the Old Testament. The word "<u>riches</u>" is mentioned (materially) *seventy-two times* in the Old Testament and *seven times* in the Gospels, for a total of *seventy-nine times. Zero times spiritually* in the Old Testament. <u>"Richer"</u> is mentioned *one time* (materially) in the Old Testament and *zero times* in the Gospels, and *zero times (spiritually)* in the Old Testament.

"Richly" is mentioned *0 times* (materially or spiritually) in the Old Testament. "Enrich" is mentioned *2 times* (materially) in the Old Testament, *none* in the Gospels, and *none spiritually*. The word "enriched" is mentioned *not once* (materially or *spiritually)* in the Old Testament. "Enriches" is mentioned (materially) *1 time* in the Old Testament and *none* spiritually. "Wealth" is mentioned (materially) *25 times* in the Old Testament, *none spiritually*. "Wealthy" is mentioned (materially) *2 times* in the Old Testament, *none spiritually*. All of these words are mentioned for a *total of 157 times materially in the Old Testament, which includes the Gospels, and only twice spiritually.*

In the New Testament the word "rich" is mentioned (materially) *seven times negatively* and *nine times (spiritually) all positively.* The word "riches" is mentioned (materially) *three times,* twice negatively and once positively. It is mentioned *fourteen times (spiritually) all positively.* Here are all the Scriptures concerning the word "riches" in the New Testament. Romans 2:4: "Or despises the riches of his *goodness* [spiritual] and *forbearance* [spiritual] and *longsuffering* [spiritual]." *Spiritual riches* is what he is speaking about, the riches of His goodness, forbearance and longsuffering, and not the riches of financial things. Romans 9:23: "And that he might make known the riches of his *glory* [spiritual] on the vessels of mercy [that is us], which he had afore prepared unto glory." Romans 11:12; "Now if the fall of them [Israel] be the *riches of the world* and the diminishing of them the *riches of the Gentiles . . .*" Verse 11: "I say then, have they stumbled that they should fall? God forbid: but rather *through their fall salvation is come unto the Gentiles,* for to provoke them [Israel] to jealousy." Salvation came to us through their unbelief. Romans 11:33: "O the depth of the riches both of the *wisdom* [spiritual] and *knowledge* [spiritual] of God! . . ." Ephesians 1:7: "In whom we have redemption through his blood, the forgiveness of sins, according to the riches of his *grace* [spiritual]." Ephesians 1:18, ". . . what the riches of the *glory* [spiritual] of his inheritance . . ." Ephesians 2:7: "That in the ages to come he might shew the exceeding riches of his *grace* [spiritual] in his kindness toward us through Christ Jesus." Ephesians 3:8: ". . . I should preach among the Gentiles the unsearchable riches of *Christ."* Ephesians 3:16: ". . . the riches of his *glory* [spiritual] . . ." Philippians 4:19: ". . . supply all your need [both material and spiritual] according to his riches in *glory* [spiritual] by Christ Jesus." Colossians 1:27: ". . . what is the riches of the *glory* [spiritual] of this mystery . . ." Colossians 2:2: ". . . together in love, and unto all riches of the *full assurance* [spiritual] of understanding . . ." Hebrews 11:26: ". . . the *reproach of Christ* [spiritual] greater riches than . . ."

To sum this up, the appearance of the words "richer," "richly," "enrich," "enriched," "enriches," "wealth," and "wealthy" is as follows:

Richer is mentioned *zero times* in the New Testament.

Richly is mentioned *two times* in the New Testament; it was spoken of positively *once spiritually* and *once materially* in 1 Timothy 6:17.

Enrich is mentioned *zero times* in the New Testament.

Enriched is mentioned *twice positively (materially)* in the New Testament.

Enriches is mentioned *zero times* in the New Testament.

Wealth is mentioned *two times* in the New Testament, *one time (materially) negatively,* and *one time (spiritually) positively.*

Wealthy is mentioned *zero times.*

So, where are we getting all of this teaching on prosperity, money, riches, and wealth from? <u>People are saying what other people are saying, and they are using the Old Testament Scriptures, which Truth # 3 shows as being symbols, copies, patterns, figures, shadows, and examples.</u> If we are going to rely on what the Old Testament says for how we are to live today, we should also go back to performing animal sacrifices. No! The animal sacrifices were Old Testament ways to worship God. Jesus is the spiritual sacrifice, once and for all. The Old Testament material, financial, and physical things are done away with in Christ. Read 2 Corinthians 3:6-14. *Fourteen times in the New Testament* the words, rich, riches, richer, richly, enrich, enriched, enriches, wealth, and wealthy (materially) are written. Only *four times positively, ten times negatively.* This blows me away (symbolically).

For proof, I reiterate, go <u>buy yourself a concordance.</u> Don't go around quoting what other people are saying without studying the

Bible. I don't and am using a concordance now for this book. In the Old Testament, these words concerning material things are written *157 times;* these words were spoken of (spiritually) *only twice* in a negative way. In the New Testament, these words are mentioned (materially) *only 14 times,* and *only 4 are in a positive manner.* The *other 10 occurrences are negative.* When I looked at these words in the concordance, it just blew me away, that it was 10 to 4 negative (material) occurrences in the New Testament.

So, where is all the New Testament prosperity teaching information coming from; it is coming from the Old Testament (Genesis 1:1 thru Acts 1:26). If this is so, I repeat, do we need to have animal sacrifices and do we need to build altars? Do we need to have an earthly high priest? If we want to stay under the Old Testament, we should still be keeping the Passover and we need to let the earthly high priest represent us. No! No! No! All of these things were just symbols, copies, shadows, and examples that were done away within Jesus.

I, therefore, submit to you the key point in Truth # 4, where I've demonstrated to you that the numerous times the words prosper, prosperous, rich, riches, wealth, wealthy, etc. are mentioned in the Old Testament (including the Gospels), they are referring to material and financial things. These words occur for a total of *89 times.* Yet, they only occur *4 times* in the New Testament, twice materially and twice spiritually. The word "money" is mentioned *131 times* in the Old Testament and *only 7 times* in the New Testament, *only once* in a positive way. The words rich, wealth, etc. are mentioned *159 times* in the Old Testament: 157 times materially and only twice spiritually. However, the words "rich" and "wealth" are mentioned for a total of *25 times* in the New Testament, all spiritually and all positively.

Another key point is that in the Old Testament, these words occur in *abundance* concerning material and financial things, but yet, *little* is indicated concerning spiritual things. In the New Testament these same words occur in *abundance* in reference to spiritual things and *almost no positive references* materially and/or financially (only six instances of positive occurrences out of a total of forty-three occurrences of these words). Do you see the pattern of the Holy Spirit that is evolving here? Do you see the plan of the Holy Spirit?

CHAPTER 6

Truth # 5:

Jesus' Ministry Consisted Mainly of Salvation, Healing, and Casting Out Demons: Not Once Did Jesus Make Anyone Financially Rich

There are an abundance of Scriptures about Jesus as the Savior (salvation). Through salvation, Jesus not only <u>saves</u> us from the *wrath of God's judgment,* but He <u>saves</u> us from *living in sin.* Sin brings torment, pain, hurt, and death. Salvation in Jesus brings peace, healing—relief over pain, victory over hurt, and life. Jesus delivered us from our sins so that we could live a life of holiness. In healing you have miracles. Casting out demons includes healing and miracles. Of the three major areas of the work of Jesus, which do you believe received the most Scriptures? Salvation does . . . that is why Jesus died. He died to save us from our sin and from the lake of fire, so that we can spend eternity with Him. Jesus also came to heal us. It was out of <u>compassion </u>that He was moved to *heal people from sickness* and *disease.* He came to <u>destroy the works of the devil</u> and *to cast out demons.*

The three major works of Jesus—salvation, healing, and casting out demons—is what Jesus taught; this is what the gospel is all about. Jesus spoke about the *coming of the Holy Ghost* (the Comforter) and the *future things to come.* You cannot get saved without the Holy

Spirit. You cannot get healed without the Holy Spirit and you cannot cast out demons without the Holy Spirit working in your life. He also spoke about the *end times,* the things that will come upon this world. He met the people's needs—spiritual, physical and material. He did not make anyone wealthy, rich, or a millionaire; He met their need.

Let me bring to your attention the fishing story in Luke 5:6-10, when the nets were breaking. When Jesus met the need of the fishermen (to catch fish), they had more than enough fish, so much so that the boat started to sink. They did not have a boat like an aircraft carrier, nor a battleship, where they filled it with so much fish that they could become millionaires. They had a normal-sized fishing boat. I have a brother in Slidell, Louisiana, who used to have a fishing boat, and if he would have overfilled it, it would have sunk. It would have made him neither wealthy nor rich. Although, he would have had a very good sum of money, he would not have been wealthy. Jesus met the need of the fishermen and He gave them more than enough.

Let us look at the Gospel of Matthew, since it is the first of the four Gospels, concerning verses on salvation, healing, and casting out of demons. There is <u>not a single verse</u> where Jesus made anyone rich or wealthy. Matthew 1:21 says, ". . . she shall bring forth a son and thou shall call his name Jesus, for he shall save his people from their sins" (salvation). In Matthew 2:2, Herod says, "where is he that is born King of the Jews? For we have seen his star in the east, and are come to worship him" (have come to seek the Savior, seek salvation). We are not to worship anyone except God. He is the Savior and He came to save us. Matthew 2:6: "And thou Bethlehem in the land of Juda art not the least among the princes of Juda: for out of thee shall come a Governor, that shall rule my people Israel [provide salvation]." Jesus is the Messiah; He is going to rule. He has the authority to rule and reign over Israel. Matthew 3:2 (John the Baptist preaching): "Repent ye, for the kingdom of heaven [salvation] is at hand." Jesus is ever present.

The Bible says in Matthew 3:12, "Whose fan is in his hand . . . he will thoroughly purge his floor. And gather his wheat [provide salvation] into the garner; but he will burn up the chaff with unquenchable fire." Jesus is going to gather His wheat (the saints) into His barn, and He is going to burn up the ungodly (the sinners) with unquenchable fire. Matthew 3:16: "And Jesus when he was baptized, went up straightway out of the water and lo the heavens were opened unto him, and he saw the Spirit of God descending like a dove, and lighting upon him" (salvation). Verse 17: "And lo a voice from heaven saying, this is my beloved Son, in whom I am well pleased" (salvation).

Matthew 4:16 says, "The people who sat in darkness saw great light [Jesus, the Savior] and to them which sat in the region and shadow of death light [salvation] is sprung up." The Light has come unto the Gentiles. Verse 17: "From that time Jesus began to preach and to say, Repent, for the kingdom of heaven [salvation] is at hand." He was telling them, "I am here on this earth." Verse 19: "And he said unto them, Follow me [pursue salvation], and I will make you fishers of men." In essence, Jesus was telling them, "I am the Savior, and it is the souls of men (not fish) that you are going to catch." Verse 23: "Jesus went about all Galilee, teaching in their synagogues, preaching the gospel of the kingdom [salvation], and healing <u>all manner of sickness and all manner of disease</u> among the people" (healing). Verse 24: "And his fame went throughout all Syria, and they brought to him all sick people [for healing] that were taken with divers diseases and torments, and those which were possessed with devils [demons]."

In Matthew 5:3, Jesus tells us how to live a life of holiness. "Blessed are the <u>poor in spirit</u> for theirs is the kingdom of heaven" (salvation). In Mathew chapters 5 and 6, Jesus teaches the people how to live for God; that is, the type of lifestyle we today should live. Matthew 7:13 says, "Enter ye in [obtain salvation] at the strait gate" . . . because that is how you are going to get into the kingdom of God. Jesus is the only Savior. ". . . for wide is the gate, and broad is the way that leadeth to destruction and many there be which go in thereat." Matthew 7:21: "Not every one that saith unto me, Lord, Lord . . ." has salvation. Verse 22: "have we not prophesied in thy name [Jesus' name]?" Verse 23: "And then will I profess unto them I [salvation] never knew you." In John 14:6, "Jesus saith unto him, I am the way, the truth, and the life: no man cometh unto the Father, but by me." <u>No one will get into God's kingdom without having Jesus as Lord and Savior of their lives!</u>

We evidence Jesus' works of healing in Matthew 8:2: "And behold, there came a leper and worshipped him, saying, Lord if thou wilt, thou canst make me clean [healed]." Verse 3: "And Jesus put forth his hand, and touched him, saying, I will; <u>be thou clean</u> [healed]. . . ." Verse 4: "And Jesus said unto him, See thou tell no man; *but go thy way, show thyself to the priest and offer the gift that Moses commanded, for a testimony unto them.*" The four Gospels are under the Old Testament, which commanded the people of Israel according to the law of Moses.

This is the story about the centurion's servant who was sick. Jesus said in verse 7, "I will come and <u>heal him</u>" (healing). Verse 8: "The centurion answered and said, Lord, I am not worthy that you should come under my roof; but speak the word only, and my servant <u>shall be healed</u>" (healing). Verse 13: "And Jesus said unto the centurion, Go thy way; and as thou hast believed, so be it done unto thee. And his servant was <u>healed</u> in the selfsame hour" (healing). Verse 14: "And when Jesus was come into Peter's house, he saw his wife's mother laid, and sick of a fever." Peter was married. Verse 15: "And he touched her hand, and the <u>fever left her</u> [healing took place] and she arose and ministered to them." Verse 16: "When the even was come, they brought unto him many that were possessed with devils [demons]: and he <u>cast out the spirits with his word</u>, and healed all that were sick" (healing).

Threaded throughout the Gospels, there is continued evidence of Jesus' ministry of salvation, healing, and casting out of demons. In Matthew 8, verse 17, it says, "That it might be fulfilled which was spoken by Esaias the prophet, saying, Himself took our infirmities and bare our sicknesses" (healing). Verse 22: "But Jesus said unto him, Follow me (salvation); and let the dead [spiritually] bury their dead" (physically). Follow me because I have eternal life—this is what He was telling them. *Let the spiritually dead (those that do not know Jesus) bury the physically dead.* Verse 26: ". . . Then he arose and rebuked the winds and the sea; and there was a great calm" (salvation). Only God can control the winds and the storms of the sea. Only God can give eternal life.

Verse 28: ". . . into the country of the Gergesenes, there met him two possessed with devils [demons], coming out of the tombs, exceeding fierce, so that no man might pass by that way." Verse 29: "And, behold, they cried out, saying, What have we to do with thee, Jesus, thou Son of God [salvation]? art thou come hither to torment us [demons] before the time?" Verse 31: "So the devils [demons] besought him, saying, If thou cast us out, suffer us to go away into the herd of swine." Verse 32: "And he said unto them, Go. And when they were come out, they [demons] went into the herd of swine: and, behold, the whole herd of swine ran violently down a steep place into the sea, and perished in the waters." Verse 33: "And they that kept them fled, and went their ways into the city, and told every thing, and what was befallen to the possessed of the devils" (demons).

Matthew 9:2 "And behold, they brought to him a man sick of the palsy, lying on a bed: and Jesus seeing their faith said unto the sick of the palsy; Son, be of good cheer; thy sins be forgiven thee" (salvation). Verse 5: "For whether is easier, to say, Thy sins be forgiven thee [salvation]; or to say, Arise, and walk [healing]?" Verse 6 "But that ye may know that the Son of man hath power on earth to forgive sins [salvation] (then saith he to the sick of the palsy,) Arise, take up thy bed, and go unto thine house" (healing). Verse 9: ". . . and he saith unto him, Follow me [seek salvation] . . ." Verse 13: "But go ye and learn what that meaneth, I will have mercy, and not sacrifice [the Old Testament sacrifice of animals]: for I am not come to call the righteous, but sinners to repentance" (salvation). Only Jesus has the authority to call sinners to repent. <u>Without Jesus, neither Mohammad, you, nor I can call a sinner to repent.</u> We needed to repent ourselves! Without Jesus, we have no Savior! He came because He is the Savior.

Continuing on with Scriptures on healing, in Matthew 9:20, it says, "And, behold, a woman, which was diseased with an issue of blood twelve years, came behind him, and touched the hem of his garment." She was seeking healing. Verse 21: "For she said within herself, If I may but touch his garment, I shall be whole [healed]." Verse 22: "But Jesus turned him about, and when he saw her, he said, Daughter, be of good comfort; thy faith hath made thee whole [healed]. And the woman was made whole [healed] from that hour."

He raised the dead, and he also healed them. Matthew 9:25: "But when the people were put forth, he went in, and took her by the hand, and the maid arose [she was healed]." If you are dead, you are not going to get up unless you are healed also. For example, if a person died of a bullet wound and was shot in his heart, he would have to have a miracle to survive. His heart must be healed. You have to have miracles!

Matthew 9:27: ". . . two blind men followed him, crying, and saying, Thou son of David, have mercy on [heal] us." Verse 28: "And when he was come into the house, the blind men came to him [seeking healing]: and Jesus saith unto them, Believe ye that I am able to do this? . . ." Verse 29: "Then touched he their eyes, saying, According to your faith, be it [healing] unto you." Verse 30: "And their eyes were opened [healing]; and Jesus straitly charged them, saying, See that no man know it." Verse 31: "But they, when they were departed, spread aboard his fame in all that country." Verse 32: "As they went out, behold, they brought to him a dumb man possessed with a devil" (demon). Verse 33: "And when the devil [demon] was cast out [healed], the dumb spake: [You need the power of God present to cast out demons.] and the multitudes marveled, saying, It was never so seen in Israel." In verse 35, as the testimony of his works preceded him, ". . . Jesus went about all the cities and villages, *teaching* in their synagogues, and *preaching* the gospel [salvation] of the kingdom, and healing every sickness and every disease among the people" (healing).

Jesus asks the Father to impart unto to His disciples His anointing—that is, His works of salvation, healing, and casting out demons. In Matthew 9:38: "Pray ye therefore the Lord of the harvest, that he will send forth labourers [salvation] into his harvest." Matthew 10:1: "And when he had called unto him his twelve disciples, he gave them power against unclean spirits [demons], to cast them out, and to heal all manner of sickness and all manner of disease" (healing). Verse 6: "But go rather to the lost sheep of the house of Israel" (salvation). Verse 7: "And as ye go, preach, saying, the kingdom of heaven is at hand" (salvation). Verse 8: "Heal the sick, cleanse the lepers [healing], raise the dead, cast out devils [demons]: freely ye have received, freely give." Verse 18: "And ye shall be brought before governors and kings for my sake [salvation] for a testimony against them and the Gentiles."

There is going to be a testimony. When you give a testimony, you tell what great things God has done for you. <u>You are testifying before the people: "Jesus is my Savior!</u> He delivered me, and He is my healer!" Matthew 10:22: "And ye shall be hated of all men for my name's sake: but he that endureth to the end shall be saved" (salvation). *You will he hated* because of Jesus. Verse 32: "Whosoever therefore shall confess me [salvation] before men, him will I confess also before my Father which is in heaven." *You will have eternal life.* Verse 37: "He that loveth father or mother more than me [salvation] is not worthy of me: and he that loveth son or daughter more than me is not worthy of me." Verse 38: "And he that taketh not his cross [does not pursue salvation], and followeth after me, is not worthy of me" (salvation). Verse 39: "He that findeth his life shall lose it: and he that loseth his life for my sake [salvation] shall find it."

Matthew 11:5: "The blind receives their sight, and the lame walk, the lepers are cleansed, and the deaf hear [healing], . . . the dead are raised up, and the poor have the gospel preached to them" (salvation). Verse 27: "All things are delivered unto me of my Father [salvation]: and no man knoweth the Son, but the Father; neither knoweth any man the Father, save the Son, and he to whomsoever the Son will reveal him" (salvation). Verse 28: Come "unto me, all ye that labour and are heavy laden, and I will give you rest" (salvation).

Only God can give us true rest! He is greater than the Sabbath. In Matthew 12:6, it says, "But I say unto you, That in this place is one greater than the temple" (salvation)." Verse 8: "For the Son of man is Lord even of the sabbath day" (salvation). Verse 10: "And, behold there was a man which had his hand withered. And they asked him, saying is it lawful to heal on the sabbath days? That they might accuse him" (healing). Verse 13: "Then saith he to the man, Stretch forth thine hand. And he stretched it forth; and it was restored whole, like as the other" (healing). Verse 15: "But when Jesus knew it, he withdrew himself from thence: and great multitudes followed him, and he healed them all" (healing). Verse 18: "Behold my servant, whom I have chosen; my beloved, in whom my soul is well pleased: I will put my spirit upon him, and he shall shew judgment to the Gentiles" (God has chosen Jesus as our salvation). Verse 21: "And in his name shall the Gentiles trust" (salvation).

This is the gospel of Jesus! There are many scriptures on salvation because Jesus came to save us. This is why some evangelists are successful, as they preach salvation above everything else. *Jesus came to save us from our sins so we won't continue living in sin.* God means business; He does not take sin lightly. Matthew 11:22: "Then was brought unto him one possessed with a devil [demon] blind and dumb: and he healed him [healing] . . . insomuch that the blind and dumb both spake and saw." Verse 28: "But if I cast out devils [demons] by the Spirit of God, then the kingdom of God [salvation] is come unto you." Verse 40: "For as Jonas was three days and three nights in the whale's belly; so shall the Son of man be three days and three nights in the heart of the earth" (salvation). Jesus died and was raised up to save us! Verse 41: "The men of Nineveh shall rise in judgment with this generation, and shall condemn it; because they repented at the preaching of Jonas; and behold, a greater [Jesus—our salvation] than Jonas is here." We need to repent: "I am your Savior" is what Jesus is telling us!

Matthew 11:42: "The queen of the south shall rise up in the judgment with this generation, and shall condemn it: for she came from the uttermost parts of the earth to hear the wisdom of Solomon: and behold, a greater than Solomon [salvation] is here." She is going to witness against them in the day of judgment. Verse 43: "When the unclean spirit [demon] is gone out of a man, he walketh through dry places, seeking rest, and findeth none." Verse 44: "Then he [demon] said I will . . ." Verse 45: "Then goeth he, and taketh with himself seven other spirits [demons] more wicked than himself, and they enter in and dwell there . . ."

Matthew 13:30: "Let both grow together until the harvest and in the time of harvest [end times]: I will say to the reapers, gather ye together first the tares, and bind them in bundles to burn them: but gather the wheat [salvation] into my barn" (God's kingdom). Verse 35: "That it might be fulfilled which was spoken by the prophet, saying, I will open my mouth in parables; I [salvation] will utter things which have been kept secret from the foundation of the world." He is the Savior, He is God! Verse 39: "The enemy that sowed them is the devil [demons]; the harvest is the end of the world; and the reapers are the angels." Verse 41: "The Son of Man shall send forth his angels, and they shall gather out of his kingdom [salvation] all things that offend, and them which do iniquity."

Matthew 14:14: "And Jesus went forth, and saw a great multitude, and was moved with compassion toward them, and he healed their sick" (healing). Verse 26: "And when the disciples saw him walking on the sea, they were troubled, saying It is a spirit . . ." Try walking on water! I don't mean by trickery. He (salvation) is walking on the sea. He is the Savior! Verse 33: "Then they that were in the ship came and *worshipped him,* saying of a truth thou art the Son of God." Jesus is our salvation, He is the Messiah. Verse 35: "And when the men of that place had knowledge of him, they sent out into all that country round about, and brought unto him all that were diseased" (healing). Verse 36: "And besought him that they might only touch the hem of his garment: and as many as touched were made perfectly whole" (healing).

In chapter 15 of Matthew, verse 22, it says, "And behold, a woman of Canaan came out of the same coasts, and cried unto him, saying, Have mercy on me, O Lord, thou son of David; my daughter is grievously vexed with a devil" (demons). Verse 24: "But he answered and said, I am not sent but unto the lost sheep of the house of Israel" (salvation). Verse 28: "Then Jesus answered and said to her, O woman, great is thy faith; be it unto thee *even as thou wilt.* And her daughter was made whole [demon] from that very hour." The demon came out of her daughter that very hour.

As a result of the works of healing that Jesus did, we see in Matthew 15, verse 30, "And great multitudes came unto him, having with them those that were lame, blind, dumb, maimed, and many others, and cast them down at Jesus' feet; and he healed them" (healing). Verse 31: "Insomuch that the multitude wondered, when they saw the dumb to speak, the maimed to be whole, the lame to walk, and the blind to see [healing]; and they glorified the God of Israel."

Matthew 16:16: "And Simon Peter answered and said, Thou art the Christ, the Son of the living God" (salvation). Verse 16 along with John 3:16 are two of the greatest revelations of the entire Bible. Verse 17: "Blessed art thou, Simon Barjona |you, I, or anyone else who has this revelation; knows it's all about Jesus, Jesus, Jesus, and nothing else!| . . . for flesh and blood |mankind| hath not revealed it unto thee, but my Father |salvation| which is in heaven." Verse 18: "And I say also unto thee, thou art Peter, and upon this rock I will build my church |salvation| and the gates of hell |demons| shall not prevail against it." No one can truly say, "I am going to build my church," except Jesus. Verse 19: "And I will give unto thee the keys of the kingdom of heaven |salvation| and whatsoever thou shalt bind on earth shall be bound in heaven . . ."

Matthew 16:21: "From that time forth began Jesus to shew unto his disciples, how that he must go unto Jerusalem, and suffer many things of the elders and chief priests and scribes, and be killed, and be raised again the third day" (salvation). Try being raised from the dead without Jesus—the Savior! In verse 23: "But he turned, and said unto Peter, Get thee behind me, Satan |demons|: thou art an offence unto me . . ." (He was telling Satan that he was not going to use Peter against Him.) Verse 24: "Then said Jesus unto his disciples, If any man will come after me, let him deny himself, and take up his cross, and follow me" (salvation). Verse 25 "For whosoever will save his life shall lose it: and whosoever will lose his life for my sake shall find it" (salvation, you better follow Him). Verse 27: "For the Son of man shall come in the glory of his Father |salvation| with his angels; and *then he shall reward every man* according to his works." Verse 28: "Verily I say unto you, There be some standing here, which shall not taste of death, till they see the Son of man coming in his kingdom" (salvation).

Matthew 17:2 says Jesus was transfigured before them: ". . . and his face did shine as the sun, and his raiment was white as the light" (perfect and holy—salvation). Verse 3: "And behold, there appeared unto them Moses and Elias |salvation| talking with him." Verse 5: "While he yet spake, behold, a bright cloud overshadowed them: and behold a voice out of the cloud, which said, This is my beloved Son, in whom I am well pleased; hear ye him" (salvation).

Verse 9: "And as they came down from the mountain, Jesus charged them, saying: Tell the vision to no man, until the Son of man be risen [resurrected] again from the dead" (salvation). <u>Only the Savior can be raised from the dead!</u>

In Matthew 17:15, it says, "Lord, have mercy on my son: for he is lunatick, and sore vexed [demon]: for ofttimes he falleth into the fire, and oft into the water." Verse 16: "And I brought him to thy disciples, and they could not cure him" (cast out the demon). Verse 18: "And Jesus rebuked the devil [demon]; and he departed out of him: and the child was cured from that very hour." Verse 23: "And they shall kill him, and the third day he shall be raised again [salvation] . . ." Chapter 18:11: "<u>For the Son of man is come to save that which was lost" (salvation).</u> Verse 12: "How think ye? If a man have an hundred sheep, and one of them be gone astray, doth he not leave the ninety and nine, and goeth into the mountains, and seeketh that which is gone astray [salvation]?" Verse 20: "For where two or three are gathered together in my name [salvation], there am I in the midst of them."

Remember, *this is the key verse to Truth # 1.* Matthew 19:28: ". . . when the <u>Son of man shall sit in the throne of his glory . . ."</u> <u>(salvation).</u> Verse 29: ". . . for my name's sake, <u>shall receive an</u> <u>hundredfold,</u> and shall inherit everlasting life" (salvation). Matthew 20:19: ". . . and the third day he shall rise again" (salvation). Verse 21: "Grant that these my two sons may sit, the one on thy right hand, and the other on the left, in thy kingdom" (salvation). Verse 28: ". . . to give his life for a ransom."

This is the story of blind men—Matthew 19:30: "And, behold, two blind men [healing] sitting . . ." Verse 33: "They say unto him, Lord, that our eyes may be opened" (healing). Verse 34: "So Jesus had compassion on them, and touched their eyes: and immediately their eyes received sight [healing], and they followed him." Matthew 21:5: "Tell ye the daughter of Sion [Jerusalem]. Behold, thy king [salvation] cometh unto thee . . ."

Here Jesus had entered into the temple. Matthew 21:13: "And said unto them, It is written, <u>My house shall be called the house of</u> <u>prayer;</u> but ye have made it a den of thieves." Verse 14: "And the blind and the lame came to him in the temple; and he healed them" (healing). Verse 32: "For John came unto you in the way of righteousness [salvation], and ye believed him not; but the publicans and the harlots believed him: and ye, when ye had seen it, repented not afterward, that ye might believe him . . ." Verse 37: "But last of all he sent unto them his son, saying, they will reverence my son" (salvation). Verse 42: ". . . The stone [Jesus] which the builders [Israel] rejected, the same is become the <u>head of the corner . . .</u>" (salvation). Verse 44: "And whosoever shall fall on this stone [Jesus] shall be broken [salvation]; but on whomsoever it shall fall, it will grind him to powder" (destroy).

Matthew 22:2: "The kingdom of heaven is like unto a certain king, which made a marriage for his son" (salvation). Verse 44: "The Lord said unto my Lord . . ." (David's Lord—salvation). Matthew 23:37: ". . . how often would I have gathered [salvation] thy children together, even as a hen gathereth her chickens under her wings, and ye would not!" Verse 39: "For I say unto you, ye shall not see me henceforth, till ye shall say, blessed is he [salvation] that cometh in the name of the Lord."

Jesus' second coming, Matthew 24:27 "For as the lightning cometh out of the east, and shineth even unto the west; so shall also the coming of the Son of man be" (salvation). Verse 30: "And then shall appear the sign of the Son of man in heaven: and then shall all the tribes of the earth mourn, and they shall see the <u>Son of man coming in the clouds of heaven with power and great glory" (salvation).</u> Verse 31: "And he shall send his angels with a great sound of a trumpet, and they shall gather together his elect [salvation] from the four winds, from one end of heaven to the other." Verse 44: "Therefore be ye also ready: for in such an hour as they think not the Son of man cometh" (salvation).

The story of the bridegroom—Matthew 25:10: "And while they went to buy, the bridegroom came; and they that were ready went in [salvation] with him to the marriage: and the door was shut." Verse 11: "Afterward came also the other virgins, saying, Lord, Lord open to us" (salvation). Verse 13: "Watch therefore, for ye know neither the day nor the hour wherein the Son of man cometh" (salvation).

Matthew 25:31 "When the Son of man shall come in his glory, and all the holy angels with him [salvation], <u>then shall he sit upon</u>

the throne of his glory." Verse 34: "Then shall the King say unto them on his right hand, Come, ye blessed of my Father, inherit the kingdom prepared for you [salvation] from the foundation of the world." Verse 40: "And the King shall answer and say unto them, Verily I say unto you, Inasmuch as he have done it unto one of the least of these my brethren, ye have done it unto me" (salvation). Verse 46: "And these shall go away into everlasting punishment: but the righteous into life eternal" (salvation).

Matthew 26:53: "Thinkest thou that I cannot now pray to my Father, and he shall presently give me more than twelve legions of angels [salvation]?" Verse 64: ". . . Hereafter shall ye see the Son of man sitting on the right-hand of power, and coming in the clouds of heaven" (salvation).

Gospel of Matthew, chapter 28, verse 7 says, ". . . and tell his disciples that he is risen from the dead [salvation] . . ." Verse 9: ". . . And they came and held him by the feet, and worshipped him" (salvation). *Only God can receive true worship.* Verse 17: "And when they saw him, they worshipped him [salvation]: but some doubted." Verse 18: "And Jesus came and spake unto them, saying, all power is given unto me in heaven and in earth" (salvation). Verse 20: "Teaching them to observe all things whatsoever, I have commanded you: and lo, I am with you alway, even unto the ends of the world" (salvation).

Whenever the scriptures above referred to Jesus as the Savior, I placed the word salvation in parenthesis. *The words the "Son of David" and the "Christ" refer to Jesus as the Messiah that Israel was expecting to come.* The Son of David is mentioned seven times (salvation), and Christ is mentioned seventeen times (salvation).

I submit to you the key point is that in the book of Matthew, salvation is mentioned in 101 verses, plus 24 (Son of David, Christ), for a *total of 125 verses;* healing is mentioned in *37 verses,* and demons are mentioned in *23 verses.* These are the main focuses of Jesus' teachings and works that we are commanded to do. There is *not a single verse* where Jesus made anyone rich. *Nor did He promise* to make anyone rich upon this earth during this age. There are other verses in Matthew, which I did not include in the count. I believe this is already an overkill (symbolic of more than enough). The Gospels of Mark, Luke, and John are likewise.

CHAPTER 7

Truth # 6:

The Law of Gravitation, Man's (Material/ Financial) in Contrasts to God's (Spiritual)

The law of gravitation consists of a spiritual law and a physical law. Today, many Christians still want to see something physical. The Bible tells us in many verses to look at the spiritual things and not the physical things. 2 Corinthians 5:7: "For we walk by faith, not by sight." 2 Corinthians 4:18: "While we look not at the things which are seen [because they are temporary], but the things which are not seen are eternal." *There is something in man that constantly causes him to gravitate to the things that are physical and material.*

In the Old Testament, long before Abraham, Abel sacrificed an animal and he built a physical altar. Abraham built altars with stones. We know that Jacob did too. We know Elijah built an altar also, when he called fire down from heaven. Moses built a tabernacle, which included the ark of the covenant. Solomon built the temple and Nebuchadnezzar destroyed it. Zerubbabel rebuilt it and Herod enlarged it. <u>God dwelled among His people then, and today He dwells within us.</u> Now all these material and physical temples were done away with because of Jesus.

We are the temple of God—1 Corinthians 3:16: "know ye not that ye are the temple of God and that the Spirit of God dwelleth in you?" We are the temple of God if we are truly born of the Spirit. The Spirit of God dwells in our spirit, which dwells in our body. When we die, the Holy Spirit does not go into the grave. The Holy Spirit dwells in our spirit, and, since our bodies house our spirit when we are alive, we are God's temple. No more focusing on physical buildings and things.

We are going to look at the Gospel of John, which occurred under the Old Testament. *In John's Gospel, men gravitated toward physical and material things.* That is what is happening today. The focus is on financial prosperity. Jesus was/is focusing and speaking about spiritual prosperity. This is what happened in the Gospel of John. I will pick one example out of each chapter, except chapters three, and four (two each); however, there are other chapters with more than one example.

We are going to start with John's Gospel, chapter 1, verse 16; however, verse 17 is the key verse. John 1:16 this is not a real strong point, but it's there: "and of his fullness [speaking about Jesus] have all we received and grace for grace." We received grace (spiritually) from the fullness of Jesus; fullness in grace is everything we get from God through grace (spiritually).

John 1:17 "For the law was given by Moses." The law of Moses had works: It was composed of (physical) outward things that Israel had to do. *The law gravitated toward the physical realm:* physical, financial, and material things, like all the sacrifices that Israel was commanded to do. Grace and truth (spiritual) was given by whom? Jesus Christ, that's who! In the Gospel, the apostle John is telling us that John the Baptist is a witness for Jesus and is saying that the fullness of God has come. We received grace for grace. We start with grace and we will finish with grace. *Grace gravitates toward the spiritual realm.* Grace, grace, grace—everything we have from God is through grace and not from the works of the law of Moses.

True Christians are perfect in Christ because Jesus is our perfection, our salvation, our righteousness, and it is because of the grace of God. Yes! Today, God calls us saints, righteous, faithful, blessed, beloved, and sons/daughters of the living God, because of the grace of

God. The church at Corinth had many problems, yet the apostle Paul called them saints, brethren, faithful, and righteous. Many people, including ministers, don't want to hear this because they focus on the lifestyle of some Christians. But that is *who true Christians are,* because of the grace of God. It is the work of Jesus that makes us saints and righteous, and not our own works. Ephesians 2:10: "<u>For we are his workmanship . . .</u>"

The law dealt with physical things like keeping the Passover. Do we keep the Passover today? No! Do we keep the Feast of Unleavened bread today? No! Do we keep the Feast of Tabernacles today? No! And so on, and on it goes. Today, God sees us without sin because of the blood of Jesus. We don't remove all of the leavened bread from our houses; neither do we keep the Jewish Passover. Christ is our Passover (1 Cor. 5:7). No! <u>Many of these Old Testament's physical, financial, and material things were fulfilled in Jesus.</u> We are not under the law of Moses for *we have ". . . a better covenant which was established upon better promises"* (Heb. 8:6).

John 2:18: "Then answered the Jews and said unto him, What sign [give us a physical sign] shewest thou unto us, seeing that thou doest these things?" They wanted to "see" something. Do you understand that it is by sight again? Verse 19: "Jesus answered and said unto them, Destroy this temple, and in the three days I will raise it up." Destroy this body that the Spirit of God dwells in, and I'm going to raise it up (spiritual). Jesus is saying come over here into the spiritual realm. Verse 20: "Then said the Jews, Forty and six years was this [physical] temple in building . . ." *Jesus was trying to get them into the spiritual realm (his body/spiritual temple) and they are focusing on the physical realm (physical temple).* That's what is happening today. <u>We are focusing on the physical realm (money) when God is trying to get us to focus on the spiritual realm</u>. They were looking at a physical temple, and Jesus was trying to get them into the spiritual realm; "Destroy this temple and in three days I will raise it up" (spiritual temple of God)). Constantly, He said that the Son of man will be crucified and in three days, He will rise again.

Peter said he would fight for Jesus, but He "said unto Peter, Get thee behind me Satan,"because Peter was looking at the physical realm. *I have to give my body, the temple of God to redeem mankind,"* *yet Peter and the Jews were focusing on the natural (physical).*

In John's gospel, chapter 3, verse 1, "There was a man of the Pharisees named Nicodemus, a ruler of the Jews." Verse 2: "The same came to Jesus by night . . ." Verse 3: "Jesus answered, and said unto him, Verily, verily I say unto thee, Except a man be born again [a second time], he cannot see the kingdom of God." Now Nicodemus (mankind today) said unto Him, "How can a man be born again when he is old [physically]?" Symbolically, I'm eighty years old; can I go a second time into my mother's womb (physically)? Verse 4: ". . . How can a man be born when he is old? can he enter the second time into his mother's womb, and be born [physical]?" Verse 5: "Jesus answered, Verily, verily, I say unto thee, Except a man be born of the water [physical, your mother's water bag—first birth] . . ." There is something greater than that, and it's being born of the Spirit of God (spiritual—second birth). ". . . He cannot enter into the kingdom of God." You need to be born of the Spirit of God. Verse 6: "That which is born of the flesh is flesh [physical—mother's body] . . ." We are not going to get to heaven like that; we need to be born of God ". . . and that which is born of the Spirit is [our] spirit" (spiritually). *Nicodemus had gravitated toward the physical realm (his body). Jesus was trying to gravitate him toward the spiritual realm (the new birth).* "Nicodemus, you are not going back into your mother's womb a second time," is what Jesus was telling him. "I want you to recognize that you also must have a spiritual birth. "

I will give you two more examples in Chapter 3. In verse 14, Jesus speaks about the serpent of brass that Moses lifted up on a (physical) pole in the wilderness. Man had to *focus on a physical pole with a serpent on it to be healed(delivered). Jesus was saying that man's deliverance would come through him the Son of Man being lifted up.(spiritual)* We can also look at verses 31, 32 and 34, "...he (man) that is of the earth is earthly, and speaketh of the earth" (physical, financial and material things). Verse 32"And what he hath seen and heard (from the Father) that he (Jesus) testifieth..." (heavenly things). Verse 34 "For he whom God hath sent speaketh the words of God..." (spiritual). John was saying that man gravitates to the earthly physical things while Jesus *gravitates toward the spiritual realm.*

You have the power in your mouth to share the Gospel of Jesus Christ so that others can have spiritual wealth, eternal life. Well, one might say we need more money, NO! It's not the money, what we need is to operate more under the anointing of the Holy Spirit. There is no evil in money itself, but you can neither depend on money, nor emphasize speaking about it, nor believe that you have the power to create financial wealth. No! You have the power to create spiritual wealth, and that is to get people saved. Jesus said in Acts 1:8, "But ye shall receive power, <u>after that the Holy Ghost</u> is come upon you [<u>not after you receive more money]:</u> and ye shall be witnesses unto me . . ." God will take care of the money. The emphasis is on the spiritual, not on the material.

This is the story of the woman at the well in Samaria (John 4), where Jesus asks her to give him a drink. John 4:10: "Jesus answered and said unto her, If thou knewest the gift of God, and who it is that saith to thee, Give me to drink; thou wouldest have asked of him, and he would have given thee living water" (spiritual life). Verse 11: "The woman saith unto him, Sir, thou hast nothing [you don't have a physical bucket] to draw with . . ." Since the well is physically deep, how are you going to get any water from it? Where are you going to get this living water? She thought that He was speaking about living, physical water, but Jesus was speaking about something much more important than physical water that was in Jacob's well. Verse 13: "Jesus answered and said unto her, Whosoever drinketh of this water [physical] shall thirst again." In other words, "Woman I am not speaking about physical water"; *she had gravitated toward the physical realm.* Verse 14: "But whosoever drinketh of the water that I shall give him shall never thirst [spiritual water—you are going to have eternal life]; but the water that I shall give him shall be in him a well of water springing up into everlasting life." What kind of life? Everlasting and eternal life means the same thing. He's speaking about water that will spring up into everlasting life (spiritually). *Jesus was trying to get her to gravitate toward the spiritual realm.*

In John 4:20, the woman said "Our fathers worshipped in this [physical] mountain; and ye say, that in Jerusalem is the place where men ought to worship." You know people today are going to Jerusalem trying to get closer to God, but you don't have to go anywhere. Jesus is here. Jesus lives in you if you are a true Christian. Start speaking and believing God's Word. God confirms His Word. Hebrews 4:12 says the Bible is the living Word. It is life-giving, it is alive; it's not just words but living words. You have to start believing that God says heaven and earth shall pass away before one tittle of His Word would fail. That's why those who know me see me healed all the time. God's Word works in our lives.

There was an area where I was struggling, but we abound in some areas and we abase in others. Well, I got hold of Jesus and I told Him, "NO! NO! NO! I am tired of sin. You are Jesus and nothing is impossible with You." I rose up totally delivered, and I don't have struggles in that area any more. Praise His name! The problem is that Satan speaks to our minds, saying, "Look, look, look at the physical things, and take your eyes off of the spiritual things." *He constantly tries to gravitate us toward the material, financial, and physical (sight) realm. God tells us to gravitate toward the spiritual realm.*

John 4: 21: "Jesus saith unto her, Woman, believe me, the hour cometh, when ye shall neither in this [physical] mountain, nor yet at [physical] Jerusalem, worship the Father." Verse 23: "But the hour cometh, and now is [the words "now is" is faith speaking until the coming of the Holy Spirit], when the true worshippers shall worship the Father in spirit and in truth . . ." Not in this (physical) mountains nor in (physical) Jerusalem, but in spirit and truth (spiritual). *The woman had gravitated toward the physical, sight realm, and Jesus was trying to get her to gravitate toward the spiritual realm.* Verse 24: "God is a Spirit: and they that worship him must worship him in spirit and in truth."

You must be born again in order to truly worship God according to the Word of God, the Bible. You neither truly worship God by offering up animal sacrifices nor building rock altars anymore. No! You worship God with the fruit of your lips and from your heart (spiritually). For example, we can say, "We worship You, Lord, we glorify You, we praise You," and this is what God wants. You have to be born again to truly worship God, because if you are not, the

Bible says in John 9:31 that God does not hear sinners, except Jesus save me! They have no legal rights, but we are the children of God, and have the right to God's table.

In John 5:8, Jesus tells a man to take up his bed and walk, for the man had an infirmity for thirty-eight years. Verse 15: "The man departed, and told the Jews that it was Jesus, which had made him whole." Verse 16: "And therefore did the Jews persecute Jesus, and sought to slay him, because he had done these things on the sabbath day." On what day? The (physical) Sabbath day, but Jesus is still Lord over the Sabbath. How many of us have to keep the Sabbath today? None. Today, many churches and many denominations are still keeping the Sabbath day (physically). *Many are still functioning largely under the Old Testament, still under the law of Moses.*

Jesus is not still hanging on the cross. No! He is risen! It's the resurrection, that's what gives us life. Jesus conquered death, hell, and the grave for us. Jesus is alive! He is not still hanging on the cross. Some churches still see Jesus on the cross, as they have to see something physical. To stay under the Old Testament is to take away from the glory of Jesus' redemptive work. This is Satan's number one purpose! The Jews were concerned about the Sabbath day. That's all they were concerned about, a physical day. *They had gravitated toward the physical realm.*

John 5:17: "But Jesus answered them, My Father worketh hitherto, and I work." Jesus was saying, "I healed this man; it's a spiritual work. It took a miracle to heal him, as he had not walked in thirty-eight years." Jesus was working under His Father's authority (spiritual), but they were only concerned about the Sabbath. Verse 18: "Therefore the Jews sought the more to kill him, because he had not only broken the sabbath, but said also that God was his Father, making himself equal with God" (spiritual). *Jesus was again trying to gravitate them toward the spiritual realm.* Verse 19: "Then answered Jesus and said unto them, Verily, verily, I say unto you, The Son can do nothing of himself, but what he seeth the Father do [Now He doesn't see the Father physically, but rather sees Him spiritually.]: for what things soever he doeth, these also doeth the Son likewise" (spiritual).

John 5:39 "Search the scriptures; for in them ye think . . ." Search the what? For in them, you think. *Don't follow the crowd, I don't care how great the numbers are, follow the Bible.* Remember John the Baptist and the woman with the mite. Because you are small or poor, that doesn't necessarily mean that you are not right in God's eyes. In 2 Corinthians 10:12, Paul said we number or compare ourselves with one another, which is not wise, because we judge outwardly and that's not the way God sees it. In Mark 10:31, Jesus says, "But many that are first [we think] shall be last and the last first." Isn't that astounding? Many whom we think are first are going to be last, and many whom we think are going to be last will be first. Jesus said that!

John 6:28 "Then said they unto him [Jesus], What shall we do, that we might work the works of God?" We want to do something physical, like under the law. *Again, they had gravitated toward the physical realm.* Verse 29: "Jesus answered and said unto them, This is the work of God, that ye believe on him whom he has sent." In other words, believe in Jesus whom the Father has sent (spiritual). They wanted to do some physical work. *Jesus was still trying to get them to gravitate toward the spiritual realm.* Verse 30: "They said therefore unto him, What sign [give us something physical or a material sign so we can see] shewest thou then, that we may see, and believe thee? what dost thou work?"

John 6:31: "Our fathers did eat manna in the desert [Remember, Moses gave them manna in the wilderness. *Again, they had gravitated toward the physical realm.];* as it is written, He gave them bread from heaven to eat." It grew on the ground and it was full of vitamins and minerals. Verse 32: "Then Jesus said unto them, Verily, verily, I say unto you, Moses gave you not that bread from heaven [It was not the true bread from heaven it was earthly bread that God under the Old Testament gave Israel to eat.]; but my Father giveth you the true bread from heaven." That's Jesus. *Once again Jesus was trying to gravitate them toward the spiritual realm.* Verse 33: "For the bread of God is he [Jesus] which come down from heaven, and giveth life unto the world."

What kind of life? Eternal life, the world already has financial, material, and physical life. He came to give us life (spiritual) and it (spiritual) more abundantly. John 6:34 "Then said they unto him, Lord, evermore give us this bread." Verse 35: ". . . I am the bread of life: he that cometh to me shall never hunger [Spiritually, as you hunger again when you eat physical bread. However, He's not speaking about physical bread.]; and he that believeth on me shall never thirst" (spiritually). The same as you will thirst again when you drink physical water. You eat food and you drink water to live so that you will not die physically. He was telling them that if they would believe in Him and come to Him, then they would neither hunger nor thirst for spiritual life. They would have eternal life.

John 6:53 "Then Jesus said unto them, Verily, verily, I say unto you, Except ye eat the flesh of the Son of man, and drink his blood, ye have no life in you." Verse 58: ". . . he that eateth of this bread shall live for ever" (spiritually). Verse 60: "Many therefore of his disciples, when they heard this, said, This is an hard saying; who can hear it?" Jesus said to them in verse 63, "It is the spirit that quickeneth [spiritual]; the flesh profiteth nothing [Physically. It profits you what? Nothing! *They had gravitated toward the physical realm and Jesus was again trying to gravitate them toward the spiritual realm.]:* the words that I speak unto you, they are spirit, and they are life." They are spiritual words and they will give you eternal life. It says that many of His disciples followed him no more.

You know what? I believe Jesus purposely said this to see if they trusted in Him with all their heart. I believe that's why sometimes the answer to our prayers aren't manifested right away, because He wants to let us know whether we believe in Him for the physical manifestation of our healing or money, or do we trust Him? Are we putting our trust and confidence in Him no matter what? Verse 66: "From that time many of his disciples went back [backslidden, turned away from God], and walked no more with him." Today, many will stop going to church because they don't receive their manifestation, or they will say within themselves, "He's not doing anything for me." Consequently, they just do their own thing. He wants you to trust in Him, stay with Him, follow Him, and not backslide.

John's Gospel, chapter7, verse 37: "In the last day, that great day of the feast, Jesus stood and cried, saying, If any man thirst, let him come unto me, and drink." He was not speaking of drinking physical water. Verse 38: "He that believeth on me, as the scriptures hath said, out of his belly [his spirit] shall <u>flow rivers</u> of living water." Verse 39: "(But this spake he of the Spirit, which they that believe on him should receive: for the Holy Ghost was not yet given; because that Jesus was not yet glorified.)" He was speaking about the filling of the Holy Ghost in Acts 2:4. The world can receive Jesus (John 3:16), but the world cannot receive the Holy Ghost (John 14:17) until they receive Jesus.

He was speaking under the Old Testament about the coming of the Holy Ghost, which didn't happen until the day of Pentecost (Acts 2:1: "And they were all filled with the Holy Ghost and began to speak with other tongues."). He said, "out of his belly"; He was not speaking about physical water coming out of our belly, but about spiritual water, which shall flow like rivers of living water, the filling of the Holy Ghost. *Jesus was trying to get them to gravitate toward the spiritual realm.*

John 7:40: "Many of the people therefore, when they heard this saying, said, Of a truth this is the Prophet." Verse 43: "So there was a division among the people because of him." *Again, they had gravitated toward the physical realm.* They had division then, and that's what we have today because many people don't study the Bible for themselves in detail.

John, chapter 8, verse 51: "Verily, verily, I say unto you, If a man keep my saying, he shall never see death" (eternal damnation). Verse 52: "Then said the Jews unto him, Now we know that thou hast a devil. Abraham is dead, and the prophets; and thou sayest, If a man keep my saying, he shall never taste of death" (physical). Verse 53: "Art thou greater than our father Abraham, which is dead? and the prophets are dead: whom makest thou thyself?" *They had gravitated toward the physical realm.* Verse 56: "Your father Abraham rejoiced to see my day: and he saw it, and was glad." Verse 57: "Then said the Jews unto him, Thou art not yet fifty years old, and hast thou seen Abraham?" Verse 58: ". . . Verily, verily, I say unto you, Before Abraham was, I am." Jesus was telling them that He existed before Abraham. In other words, "I'm not the God of the dead, but of the living. Abraham, Isaac and Jacob are all alive (spiritually), because I am the God of the living." *Jesus kept trying to gravitate them toward the spiritual realm.*

In John 9, there was a man who was born blind, and His disciples wanted to know who sinned—this man or his parents? They were wondering if this man's or his parents' sin had caused him to be born blind. Jesus told them neither, because they are looking at the physical. John 9:3: ". . . Neither hath this man sinned, nor his parents: but that the works of God should be made manifest in him." Verse 4: "I must work the works of him that sent me, while it is day: the night cometh, when no man can work." *He continually tried to gravitate them toward the spiritual realm.* He was neither speaking about a physical night nor a physical day; He was speaking spiritually. Once you leave this earth, you can no longer do the works of God, you must do it now. So, I must work today (now).

John 9:5 "As long as I am in the world, I am the light of the world." (He is what?) Jesus is the light of the world. He was not speaking about a physical light, but a spiritual light. Verse 10: "Therefore said they unto him, How were thine eyes opened?" They were trying to figure this out physically. *Once again, they had gravitated toward the physical realm.*

The Jews did not believe that He had been born blind. You see they were looking for a physical explanation. They could not understand, because they were operating in the physical realm and He was doing the work of his Father. Supernaturally, He was operating in the spiritual realm. John 9:38: "And he said, Lord, I believe [spiritual]. And he worshipped him." He worshipped Jesus. It wasn't about money. It's about the fruit of our lips, worshipping God. Verse 39: "And Jesus said, For judgment I am come into this world, that they which see not [spiritually] might see; and that they which see might be made blind." The Pharisees, who thought they had it all together, were told that they were spiritually blind. Now you are accountable for your sins, which was what He was telling them.

John 10:7: ". . . I am the door of the sheep." Do you believe that He was speaking about a wooden or iron door? No! He was speaking about Himself as the Savior, the spiritual door into the kingdom of God. Verse 10: "The thief [the devil] cometh not, but for to steal, and to kill, and to destroy: I am come that they might have life [eternal life], "and that they might have it more abundantly." Not material life but eternal life (spiritual). *We have gravitated toward the material and financial realm.*

In Truth # 7, I'm going to show you that John was speaking about eternal life and neither material nor financial things. If anyone *knew what God was saying, it was John, since he wrote the Gospel of John.*

John 3:16: "For God so loved the world, that he gave his only begotten Son, that whosoever believeth in him should not perish, but have everlasting life" (eternal life). We shall have what kind of life? Everlasting (eternal) life—that's what, not physical life! In fact, we already have that. He came to give us the abundant eternal life, the fruit of the Spirit operating in our lives. *Some people think that He came to give us material and financial things.* Now, wait a minute! The fornicators, adulterers, drunkards, murders, idolaters, and effeminate (gays) have physical, material, and financial prosperity in abundance. So that can't be what He came for, since the world already had that.

No one had eternal life nor the Spirit of God dwelling in them until Jesus came. Jesus did not come to give us more money. The sinners have the majority of it. Beginning with the thousand-year reign, we're going to have it. Guess who's going to rule? Jesus! Today, Satan is the god of this world (2 Cor. 4:4). Jesus came that we might have an abundant life operating in the fruit of the Spirit, which are love, joy, peace, longsuffering, gentleness, goodness, faith, etc.

In John 11, a friend of Jesus had died, and when Jesus heard about it, He told His disciples that He would go to Lazarus. John 11:11 ". . . he saith unto them, Our friend Lazarus sleepeth; but I go, that I may awake him out of sleep." Verse 12: "Then said his disciples, Lord, if he sleep, he shall do well." *They had gravitated toward the physical realm,* because they thought that Lazarus was just sleeping. Verse 13: "Howbeit Jesus spake of his death: but they thought that he had spoken of taking of rest in sleep." Verse 14: "Then said Jesus unto them plainly, Lazarus is dead." *Jesus was trying to gravitate them toward the spiritual realm.* He was telling them that Lazarus was really dead, but death to Jesus was like taking a nap. In essence, "I am going to raise him from the dead just like you would awaken a person from sleep." In verse 43, He told Lazarus to come forth from the grave, and he did.

Again in John 12, Jesus had gone to Martha's house, where her sister Mary and their brother Lazarus were. Verse 3: "Then took Mary a pound of ointment of spikenard, very costly, and anointed the feet of Jesus . . ." Verse 5: "Why was not this ointment sold for three hundred pence, and given to the poor?" *Judas Iscariot had gravitated toward the physical realm*. Verse 7: "Then said Jesus. Let her alone: against the <u>day of my burying</u> hath she kept this." *Still, Jesus was trying to gravitate them toward the spiritual realm*.

John 13, verse 6: ". . . Peter saith unto him, Lord, dost thou wash my feet?" *Peter had gravitated toward the physical realm*. Verse 8 ". . . Jesus answered him, If I wash thee not, thou hast no part with me." Peter's feet symbolized defilement, and Jesus was telling him that He was going to cleanse him, from all of his sins, a spiritual cleaning. *Jesus was trying to gravitate Peter toward the spiritual realm*. Chapter 14:8: "Phillip saith unto him, Lord, show us the Father, and it sufficeth us." *Phillip had gravitated toward the physical realm*. He wanted to physically see the Father. Verse 9: "Jesus saith unto him . . . he that hath seen me hath seen the Father; and how sayest thou then, Show us the Father?" *Jesus was trying to gravitate Phillip and the disciples toward the spiritual realm*.

In John 15:4, Jesus said, "<u>Abide in me,</u> and I in you. As the branch cannot bear fruit of itself, except it abide in the vine; no more can ye, except ye abide in me." They understood the branch and vine, which operates in the physical realm. *Jesus was trying to gravitate them to the spiritual realm, to live in Him*. John 16:16: "A little while, and ye shall not see me and again, a little while, and ye shall see me, because I go to the Father." Verse 18: "They said therefore, what is this that he saith, a little while?" *Jesus was trying to gravitate them toward the spiritual realm, and again they had gravitated toward the physical realm*. They are reasoning and their minds cannot understand this saying.

In John 18:33, Pilate asked Jesus if he was the King of the Jews. Verse 36: "Jesus answered, My Kingdom is not of this world . . ." Verse 37: "Pilate therefore said unto him, Art thou a king then? . . ." Pilate was referring to an earthly physical kingdom that Jesus was king over. *Pilate had gravitated toward the physical realm. In verse 36, Jesus was trying to gravitate him toward the spiritual realm,* a spiritual Kingdom. Chapter 19:10: "Then saith Pilate unto him, Speakest thou not unto me? knowest thou not that I have power to crucify thee, and have power to release thee?" Pilate was speaking of physical authority over Jesus. *He had gravitated toward the physical realm.* Verse 11: "Jesus answered, Thou couldest have no power at all against me, except it were given thee from above . . ." Jesus was referring to the authority of His Father, and *was trying to gravitate him toward the spiritual realm.*

In John, chapter 20, verse 25, Thomas ". . . said unto them, Except I shall see in his hands the print of the nails, and put my finger into the print of the nails, and thrust my hand into his side, I will not believe." *Thomas also had gravitated toward the physical realm.* He refused to believe unless he physically saw Jesus. Jesus said to Thomas in verse 27, ". . . be not faithless, but believing." *Jesus was again trying to gravitate Thomas toward the spiritual realm.*

John, chapter 21, in verse 18, Jesus had told Peter that another shall bind him and carry him where he didn't want to go. He was signifying by Peter's death how he would glorify God. *Jesus was attempting to gravitate Peter toward the spiritual realm.* Verse 21: "Peter seeing him saith to Jesus, Lord, and what shall this man do?" Peter was concerned about John saying what's going to happen to him? He was trying to get into John's business. *Peter had gravitated toward the physical realm.* Verse 22: "Jesus saith unto him, If I will that he tarry till I come, what is that to thee? follow thou me." Jesus was telling Peter, "It's none of your business what I do with John. You follow me and mind your own business."

The key *point is that men gravitated toward the physical (material/financial) realm. Today, we have gravitated toward those same realms, the same as they did then.* We can see from the Scriptures that in the book of John every chapter has the law of gravitation in it. I know this is overkill; nevertheless it is 100% Bible.

John 17 has the law of gravitation in the spiritual realm, but not in the physical realm, since the entire chapter had only Jesus speaking. Physical healing is accepted because it is a main part of Jesus' ministry, which includes salvation, healing, and casting out demons (Truth # 5). *Jesus wants us to gravitate toward the spiritual realm, the same as He was trying consistently to gravitate them in John's Gospel.* He wants us to set our affections on the things above, and not on the things of this earth Col. 3:2). To seek the things above is to have the fruit of the Spirit operating in our lives, to be walking in holiness, and to be imitators of Christ.

CHAPTER 8

Truth # 7:

Jesus Came to Give Eternal Life and It (Eternal Life) More Abundantly and Not to Give Material or Financial Prosperity

John 10:10 is one of the scriptures that many claim for their abundant life of financial prosperity. We are going to see in the Scriptures that Jesus was not speaking about financial prosperity at all in verse 10. Verse 10: "The thief cometh not, but for to steal, and to kill, and to destroy: I am come that they might have life . . ." Now Jesus did not come for us to have physical life; we already had that. Jesus didn't come for us to have material things; we already had that. Jesus didn't come for people to have wealth (Herod, Pilate, Caesar Augustus, and many people already had wealth). *No one,* not a single person, had eternal life. He came so we could have eternal life and have eternal life more abundantly: That is why Jesus came! <u>The Holy Spirit is going to reveal this truth to you throughout the Gospel and Epistles of John.</u>

If anybody should know this, it is John, because who wrote the Gospel of John? John did, he also wrote the Epistles of John. So John is the one who knows what the Gospel and Epistles of John are all about. Jesus said that He came that we might have <u>life</u> (eternal life) "and we might have <u>it</u> more abundantly." Jesus came that we might have life; so that we can become born again, having eternal life, and what do we do?

We gravitate toward the financial realm (Truth # 6). This earthly money and wealth is not eternal. What did He come for us to have more abundantly? He came that we have it, eternal life, more abundantly. Some will say that includes financial prosperity, becoming rich with a lot of money and that God is going to make you wealthy, even a millionaire. Some say that God says we can create wealth with the authority of our mouths; I have heard this preached. God called us to use our mouths to be witnesses for Jesus (Acts 1:8). Let's study the word "life" throughout the Gospel and Epistles of John. I submit to you that *the word "life" refers to eternal (everlasting) life every single time, with the exception of three times physical and two times negative. Not once did it refer to financial or material life!* Why do we take the latter part of John 10:10 and say it is material and financial life? We will look closely at the Gospel and Epistles of John.

John 1:1: "In the beginning was the Word and the Word was with God and the Word was God." Verse 2: "The same was in the beginning with God." Jesus was in the beginning for all eternity with God. The Word was God. Verse 3: "All things were made by him; and without him was not anything made that was made." Verse 4: "In him was [eternal] life and the [eternal] life was the light of men." Jesus, who is eternal life, gave eternal life to men (salvation) because men dwelled in darkness with a sin nature. Now that eternal life was in Jesus, He was the only one with eternal life. No one else under the Old Testament *(not a single person except Jesus) had eternal life.*

Today, we have eternal life because of the coming of the Holy Spirit (Acts 2:1, the day of Pentecost). Jesus was the only one with eternal life because He is God! John 1:14 says, "And the Word was made flesh," 100% man. Verse 6 says, "There was a man sent from God,…" who was John the Baptist. Verse 7 says John came "to bear witness of the Light" (Jesus), *that eternal life that flows from Jesus and gives light to men;* "that all men through him might believe." Verse 8: "He was not that Light but was sent to bear witness of that Light," which is Jesus.

In John 1:9, John said "That (Jesus) was the true Light" that flows from that <u>eternal life</u> (Jesus) "which lighted every man that cometh into the world." Everyone in the world has a chance to be saved because that true Light is Jesus. John 3:15, "That whosoever believeth in him should not perish, but have <u>eternal life.</u>" *What kind of life?* Eternal life! That is what He is speaking about, eternal life that is in Jesus who shines as the Light of the world. That is why *He says we have eternal life now.* The word eternal is the same as everlasting, and it is spiritual. He says for us to let our lights shine.

John 3:16: "For God so loved the world, that he gave his only begotten Son, that whosoever believeth in him should not perish, but have <u>everlasting life.</u>" What kind of life? Everlasting means forever and forever and forever; what that means is: it lasts forever. *So the words everlasting life, eternal life, and spiritual life mean the same.* Satan, the fallen angels, and those who die without Jesus have eternal (everlasting) death, also called spiritual death. Unfortunately, the lost have that now. Notice: He said that whosoever believes in Him should not perish but have everlasting life (eternal life). <u>When we accept Jesus as our Savior, we receive eternal life!</u> Now, we have eternal life.

We don't yet appear as what we shall be. 1 John 3:2, "Beloved now we are the sons of God [*we have eternal life in us now*], and it doth not yet appear what we shall be . . ." John 3:36: "He that believeth on the Son hath <u>everlasting life . . .</u>" What kind of life? Everlasting! We will use the word eternal life when it says everlasting life "and he that believeth not the Son shall not see <u>life.</u>" What kind of life? *Eternal life!* Without Jesus, no one is going to see eternal life; He's not speaking to a rock, He's speaking to people. ". . . he that believeth not the Son shall not see <u>life</u> . . ." (eternal life). You are going to die in your sins if you do not believe that Jesus is the great I AM.

Not man, but Jesus said that. Jesus is Lord (sovereign). He is the eternal God and ". . . he that believeth not the Son shall not see <u>life;</u> but the wrath of God abideth on him" (John 3:36; the great white throne judgment of God). *He shall not see eternal life.* John, chapter 4, verse 14 speaks about the woman at the well; remember I wrote about her in Truth # 6, she was speaking about natural earthly water.

Jesus said to her, "But whosoever drinketh of the water that I shall give him shall never thirst; but the water that I shall give him shall be in him a well of water springing up into <u>everlasting life.</u>" *What kind of life?* Again, eternal life! This is what John was writing about throughout his writings.

John 10:10 says that Jesus came to give us life (eternal life), and it more abundantly. The Bible said he came that <u>we might have (eternal) life, now all of a sudden we are going to switch the word "it" (life) to the financial and material realm.</u> *Every time the word "life" is mentioned in the Gospel and Epistles of John, the Bible is speaking about eternal life, except for five times.* Chapter 4 verse 35: "Say not ye, There are yet four months, and then cometh harvest? behold, I say unto you, Lift up your eyes, and look on the fields; for they are white already to harvest." Jesus was using an example, which we could understand, the harvest of the fruit. He was not speaking about our harvesting corn, oranges, or financial prosperity; He was speaking about winning souls for the kingdom of God. Also, the Gospel of Mark, chapter 4, verses 3 through 20 are speaking about spiritual fruit; they are not speaking about financial prosperity. Read it carefully. God is going to reward us in the day of the believer's judgment.

John 4:36: "And he that reapeth receiveth wages, and gathereth <u>fruit unto life eternal</u> . . ." Unto what? Eternal life! He was speaking about us being a witness for him winning souls for Jesus, not us just being saved and then sitting in the pews. He was speaking about living a life of holiness and having the fruit of the Spirit abounding in our lives; that we would walk in the wisdom and the understanding of who we are in Christ and understanding what God has truly done for us. *Jesus made us righteous, beloved, sons/daughters, and saints of God.* <u>We are His workmanship;</u> Ephesians 2:10 says it is His works, not ours. We are ambassadors for Christ!

All Christians need to get busy and win souls for His kingdom; that's what He was speaking about, not just being saved. We have eternal life more abundantly when we let the life of Christ abound in us. We gather fruit unto what kind of life? Eternal life, not the fruit of money, wealth, nor the riches of this world that are going to perish. These are not good enough for us. 1 Peter 1:18: "Forasmuch as ye know that ye were not redeemed with the corruptible things, as silver and gold, from your vain conversation received by tradition from your fathers." Verse 19: "But with the precious blood of Christ, as of a lamb without blemish and without spot." 1 Corinthians 6:20: "For ye are bought with a price: therefore glorify God in your body, and in your spirit, which are God's."

God did promise to meet all of our need in Philippians 4:19. We are going to bring fruit unto eternal life that both he that sows, witnesses to them about Jesus, and he that reaps, the one who prays with them and leads them to salvation may rejoice together. John 4:38: "I sent you to reap that whereon you bestowed no labour, where other man laboured and ye are entered into their labour." We are workers together with God. He is not speaking about us going out to reap silver and gold out of the ground, nor about reaping apples and oranges from a tree—He was speaking about souls (spiritual). John 5:24: "Verily, verily, I say unto you, he that hears my word and believeth on him that sent me hath everlasting life, and shall not come into condemnation but is passed from death unto life"(eternal).

The Father sent Jesus and he that hears Jesus' words has everlasting life. He was not speaking about material nor financial things, but spiritual life. He has passed from spiritual death unto spiritual (eternal) life. John 5:26; "For as the Father hath life in himself; so hath he given to the Son to have life in himself." The Father has eternal life, not material or financial life, but eternal life He has given to the Son. Men have physical life and money. *Only Jesus in this world had eternal life . . .*

John 5:29: "And shall come forth; they that have done good unto the resurrection of life" (eternal life). Verse 39: "Search the scriptures for in them ye think ye have eternal life . . ." All true believers have eternal (everlasting) life: angels have eternal life, and God is eternal life. Satan and demons have eternal death! The Scripture testifies that eternal life comes from Jesus. Now, notice the kind of life, eternal life. Verse 40: "And ye will not come to me that ye might have life." What kind of life? *Jesus is eternal life!* The unbelievers who rejected him already had material and financial prosperity. So far we haven't seen a single word concerning the word "life" on financial nor material prosperity.

John 6:26: "Jesus answered them and said, Verily, verily I say unto you ye seek me not because ye saw the miracles, but because ye did eat of the loaf and were filled." They saw material bread and they gravitated toward the material realm. Today, we have gravitated toward the financial realm. Many say that we need more money and stuff—wrong! What we need is a greater manifestation of the power of God. Don't pray for money, pray for the Holy Spirit to send revival. Verse 27: "Labour not for the meat which perisheth . . ." Which what? Perishes! Food and money of this world perishes, He was not telling us not to eat, nor to have any money. He was saying for us not to focus on earthly things. Do not emphasize money; do not preach constantly about it. *God will meet our need if we seek Him.* These material and financial things will perish. One thousand years from now these things will be gone. John 6:27: ". . . but for that meat that endureth unto everlasting life, which the Son of man shall give unto you: for him hath God the Father sealed." Verse 32: "Then Jesus said unto them, Verily, verily, I say unto you, Moses gave you not that bread from heaven; but my Father giveth you the true bread from heaven." Verse 33: "For the bread of God is he which cometh down from heaven, and giveth life unto the world" (eternal life). The manna that Moses gave them in the wilderness that grew on the ground had all the minerals and vitamins that they needed. God gave it to them daily, but they did not want that, they wanted meat. Jesus said that wasn't the true bread, but His Father gave the true bread from heaven. That meant Him. He didn't come down so that we could have more money, nor an abundance of finances. I am persuaded this is being preached out of ignorance. Many preach that God wants you to be rich and wealthy. *I believe it is a deception for us to focus on money, because it takes away from the glory of what Jesus has done for us.* Also, it takes away from the power of the Holy Spirit to set people free in true freedom. Jesus came down from heaven to give His life for the world. This is why Jesus shed his blood, died, and deposited his blood in heaven on the mercy seat. No one else could have done that, so that's why we have eternal life.

In John 6:35, Jesus said unto them that <u>He is the bread of life</u>. The bread of eternal life, spiritual bread, but they thought He was speaking about something physical, which is why many stopped following him. Jesus wants us to trust in him 100 percent, even if it looks like disaster in the natural. He is well able to give us something many times better than what we would choose—a husband, a wife, a house, or a job. Many give up; they rebel against God and they quit going to church. They quit worshipping Him and they no longer read their Bible. We tie His hands, and He can't do anything until we submit to Him, trusting in Him by faith.

When He said that he who comes to Him shall never hunger and he that believes on Him should never thirst, He was speaking spiritually. <u>Believing and acting</u> on what we believe <u>is coming to God;</u> therefore we will never hunger nor thirst spiritually. Physically, we might be like the apostle Paul—hungry, at times with no food, like some Christians today. However, that is not what He was speaking of; they thought He was speaking physically, so many left him and stopped following Him. *The "Abundant Life" is <u>not</u> about money, finances, millionaires, nor wealth.*

In John 6:40, Jesus said that ". . . this is the will of him that sent me, that every one which seeth the Son [by faith, trust in Him], and believeth on him, may have <u>everlasting life:</u> and I will raise him up at the last day." He was speaking about the resurrection. Verse 47: "Verily, verily, I say unto you, He that believeth on me hath <u>everlasting life.</u>"

John 6:48: "I am that bread of <u>life.</u>" He was speaking about spiritual bread (eternal life), not the physical manna that they had in the wilderness. Verse 51: "I am the living bread [spiritual bread], which came down from heaven: if any man eat of this bread, he shall <u>live for ever</u> [*Forever, sounds like eternal life to me.*]: and the bread that I will give is my flesh [I am going to die on that cross.], which I will give for the <u>life</u> of the world" (eternal life). No one else could have done that, because no one else has eternal life abiding in them.

John 6:53: "Then Jesus said unto them, Verily, verily, I say unto you, Except ye eat the flesh of the Son of man, and drink of his blood, ye have no <u>life</u> in you" (<u>eternal life).</u> Not physically drink His blood, the law of gravitation (Truth # 6) of wanting to see something physical. Spiritually believe in Him and come to Him, if not, Jesus said that they would not have life (eternal life) in them. People had physical life, money, and wealth, but no one had eternal life. Verse 54: "Whoso eateth my flesh, and drinketh my blood, hath eternal life . . ."

In John 6:63, Jesus said "It is the spirit that quickeneth [gives life—it is spiritual]; the flesh profiteth nothing: the words that I speak unto you, they are spirit, and they are [eternal] life." Verse 68: "Then Simon Peter answered him, Lord, to whom shall we go? thou hast the words of eternal life." Not words of material nor financial things, but words of eternal life (spiritual). John 8:12: "Then spake Jesus again unto them, saying, I am the light of the world; he that followeth me shall not walk in darkness [spiritual darkness/sin], but shall have the light of life" (eternal life). In John 10:10, Jesus said, ". . . I am come that they might have life [eternal life], and they might it [eternal life] more abundantly." *Now we know that in writing, the word "it" refers to the previous word "life" in this verse.* Not physical life, not material life, nor financial life, but eternal life more abundantly. *There is nothing in this verse about finances, and neither is there going to be anything about finances concerning the word "life" throughout the writings of John.*

I believe that over 95 percent of the Christians who gave up everything for Jesus never became rich, or wealthy, and certainly not millionaires. We are already rich in Jesus Christ, with far greater riches than the financial riches of this world. John 10:11: "I am the good shepherd: the good shepherd giveth his life for the sheep." Jesus is without sin and is eternal life. Romans 6:23 ". . . the gift of God is eternal life through Jesus Christ our Lord." John 10:15: "As the Father knoweth me, even so know I the Father and I lay down my life, for the sheep" (His life for us). John 10:17: "Therefore doth my Father love me, because I lay down my life, that I might take it again" (eternal life). John 10:28: "And I give unto them eternal life." John 11:24: "Martha saith unto him, I know that he shall rise again in the resurrection at the last day." In verse 25, "Jesus saith unto her, I am the resurrection and the life: he that believeth in me, though he were dead, yet shall he live" (eternal life). Verse 26: "And whosoever liveth and believeth in me shall never die . . ."

Jesus gives us eternal life; we will die physically, but spiritually we will never die. In John 12:25, Jesus tells us he that loves his self-centered, material, financial, physical life on this earth shall lose his life. And he that hates his life in this world and follows Jesus shall keep it unto <u>life eternal</u>. Verse 26: "If any man serve me, let him follow me . . ." Verse 50—Jesus is speaking (red letters): "And I know that his commandment is <u>life everlasting</u>: whatsoever I speak therefore, even as the Father said unto me, so I speak."

In John 14:6, Jesus said, "I am the way, the truth and <u>the life</u>: no man cometh unto the Father, but by me" (eternal life). John 17:2: "As thou hast given him power over all flesh, that he should give <u>eternal life</u> to as many as thou hast given him." Verse 3: "This is <u>life eternal</u>, that they might know thee the only true God and Jesus Christ, whom thou hast sent." John 20:31: "But these are written, that ye might believe that Jesus is the Christ [Anointed One], the Son of God; and that believing ye might have <u>life</u> through his name" (eternal life).

1 John 1:1: "That which was from the beginning, which we have heard, which we have seen with our eyes, which we have looked upon, and our hands have handled, of the <u>Word of life</u>" (eternal life). Verse 2: "(For the <u>life</u> was manifested, and we have seen it, and bear witness, and shew unto you that <u>eternal life</u>, which was with Father, and was manifested unto us ;)." 1 John 2:25: "And this is the promise that he hath promised us, even <u>eternal life</u>." In 1 John 3:14, John writes, "That we know that we have passed from [spiritual] death unto <u>eternal life</u> because we love the brethren. He that loveth not his brother abides in spiritual death." Verse 15: "Whosoever hateth his brother is a murderer: and ye know that no murderer has <u>eternal life</u> abiding in him." In verse 16, Jesus told us that we could perceive the love of God, because *He laid down his <u>life</u> for us* and *we ought to be willing to lay down our physical lives for our brethren. This is the love of God.* 1 John 5:11: "And this is the record, that God hath given to us <u>eternal life</u>, and this <u>life</u> is in his Son." Verse 12: "He that hath the Son hath <u>life</u>: and he that has not the Son of God has not <u>life</u>" (eternal life). They are living in spiritual death. Verse 13: "These things have I written unto you that believe on the name of the Son of God; <u>that ye may *know* that ye have eternal life</u>, and that you may

believe on the name of the Son of God." Verse 16: ". . . and he shall give him <u>life</u> for them . . ."(eternal life). Verse 20: "And we know that the Son of God is come, and hath given us an understanding, that we may know him that is true, and we are in him that is true, even in his Son Jesus Christ. This is the true God, and <u>eternal life.</u>"

The <u>key</u> point is that we have covered every instance of the word "life" in the Gospel and Epistles of John. The word "life" appeared for a total of *fifty-six times,* forty-one times in the gospel and fifteen times in the epistles. *Fifty-one times* it refers to <u>eternal (everlasting) life.</u> *Twice* it speaks about Peter giving his physical life for Jesus (John 13:37, 38). *Once it*'s mentioned about a man giving his physical life for a friend (John 15:13). *Twice* the word "life" was spoken in a negative way (John 12:25): A person loving his own life more than Jesus shall lose it, and 1 John 2:16 spoke of the pride of life, which is of the world. <u>Not once</u> was "life" used in reference to material or financial blessings of the believer. It is evidently true that the words "<u>life</u>" and "<u>it</u> more abundantly" <u>(life)</u> in John 10:10 refer to *eternal life (spiritually)* —salvation, the fruit of the Spirit, the life of Christ, and the love of God abounding in our lives. This is the abundant life in John 10:10.

CHAPTER 9

Truth # 8:

Jesus Told Us to Lay Up Treasures in Heaven and Not Upon This Earth

We have preached that by using our faith, we can bring our blessings down from heaven to this earth. The Bible teaches that even when we get saved, our salvation is not in heaven; it is already on this earth. Romans 10:8 says that our salvation is *in our mouth and in our heart*. However, the rewards we get for our works are being stored in heaven, but we receive our salvation upon this earth.

Matthew 6:19: "Lay not up for yourselves treasures upon earth [material blessings, finances, wealth, and riches on this earth], where moth and rust does corrupt, and where thieves break through and steal." I have heard of people investing in ministries and even the ministers stole the people's money—millions of dollars. These ministers were thieves. Are there thieves in heaven? No! They are here on this earth. Our rewards are still in heaven. The ones who are preaching that God wants us to have our rewards today are receiving their rewards now. That is their reward, which is why Jesus said, "Many that are first shall be last; and the last shall be first" (Matt. 19:30).

Those who are not receiving their rewards now are going to be first because they are storing them up in heaven. Matthew 6:20: "But lay up for yourselves treasures in heaven, where neither moth nor rust doth corrupt, and where thieves do not break through nor steal." Do not lay up your treasures upon this earth where thieves, moth, and rust are going to get hold of it, because these are temporary things; they are going to pass away, as they are corrupt. The eternal things are forever. Verse 21: "For where your treasure is, there will your heart be also."

When we hear people constantly speaking about financial and material things, this is their treasure in this life. What we are constantly speaking about is in our hearts, and that is our treasure, and what we value above all things. Matthew 12:34 says, "for out of the abundance of the heart the mouth speakth." Our love for Jesus and one another, the greatness of God, living a life of holiness, living for Jesus—these are the things that we should constantly be speaking about. But *if we are constantly speaking about money, that is what is in the abundance of our hearts.* That is our treasure and what we value most. It is of this earth, because money is of this earth.

Jesus said we cannot serve God and the riches of this world too. Matthew 6:24: "No man can serve two masters . . ." Some will say, "I can have the riches of this world and I can still serve Jesus," yet Jesus says we would hate the one and love the other. We are going to love one above the other. *We are going to serve and constantly speak about the things of God or the things of this world.* This is a choice that we will have to make. He did not say that we are going to love both. He said that we would hold to the one, and despise the other. We cannot serve God and mammon (the riches of this world).

God did promise to meet our *need* if we put Him first and not the riches and wealth of this world. Matthew 6:31: "Therefore take no thought [to be anxious, to focus or dwell on], saying, What shall we eat? {Don't be seeking material houses, cars, or financial things} or, What shall we drink? or, Wherewithal shall we be clothed?" Verse 32: *"(For after all these things do the Gentiles seek . . ."* Do the Gentiles seek after these things? You can bet your last dollar that they go after these things. Material and financial things are their idols. He said for us not to seek after things. ". . . For your heavenly

Father knoweth that ye have *need* of all these things" (Matt. 6:32) This sounds like Philippians 4:19: "My God shall supply all <u>your need.</u>" He did not say greed; he did not say He was going to make us millionaires. God is going to meet our need. Just like He met the need of the five thousand men with fish and bread. They were all fed, with twelve baskets left over. He did not make them wealthy, their need was met, however, *not a single person became rich nor wealthy.* We don't have to seek after them; nor do we have to ask for them.

In Matthew 6:33, He told us to <u>seek first the kingdom of God and His righteousness (spiritual); and all these things that we *need* shall be given or added unto us.</u> God will give us these things (food, money, clothes); we don't have to seek them. In verse 34, Jesus told us not to take anxious thought (to focus; to dwell on) for tomorrow, for tomorrow shall take thought for the things of itself. We are going to deal with tomorrow, tomorrow. ". . . Sufficient unto the day is the evil thereof" (Matt. 6:34). In other words, we have enough challenges, situations, and troubles facing us today without our worrying about tomorrow.

The world is building temporary empires of financial and material things on this earth, and today many Christians are telling people we need to do the same. *We will receive our eternal rewards after the rapture of the church.* There is going to be a believer's judgment in heaven (2 Cor. 5:10). Jesus is going to judge our works in heaven; we will be rewarded. Meanwhile, the people on earth will be going through the great tribulation, a time of great sorrow.

Then we will come back with Jesus to reign with Him on this earth (Rev. 5:10). Then will we receive houses and lands, etc, to have in the thousand- year reign of Christ (millennium). We are heirs of God and joint heirs with Christ (Rom. 8:17); everything that God has is also ours. He is going to reward every man according to his works. Our works (living for Jesus) will get us rewards, and we will reign with him for a thousand years.

We have seen that our salvation is not in heaven but in our mouths and hearts. Romans 10:6: "But the righteousness [of God] which is of faith [faith is not in heaven, it is here] speaketh on this wise, Say not in thine heart, Who shall ascend into heaven? (that is, to bring Christ down from above:).” God’s Word is already in the earth. He already came down and finished His work. <u>His authority and power is in our mouths and in our hearts.</u> *Salvation is a gift and not of works*. Verse 7: “Or who shall descend into the deep? That is to bring Christ up again from the dead.” He has already done that. Verse 8: “. . . The word is nigh thee, even in thy mouth and in thy heart . . .” Where are we? We are on this earth. He said salvation is in this earth; it is in our hearts and in our mouths.

Remember, salvation is a gift. Ephesians 2:8: “For by grace are ye saved through faith; and that not of yourselves: it is the gift of God.” Verse 9: “Not of works lest any man should boast.” *Salvation is a gift, but your rewards are because of your works (1 Cor. 3:14).* Romans 10:8: “. . . that is the word of faith, which we preach.” It is already on this earth—it is not in heaven. Verse 9: “That <u>if thou shall confess with thy mouth the Lord Jesus, and shalt believe in thine heart that God hath raised him from the dead [the resurrection of Jesus] thou shall be saved.</u>” Verse 10: “For with the heart man [who is on this earth] believeth unto righteousness, and with the mouth confession is made unto salvation.” It is on this earth.

Romans 10:17: “So then faith cometh by hearing, and hearing by the word of God.” But the word of God was preached on this earth, from way back from the beginning of time when God sent out His word through His prophets. Verse 18: “But I say, have they not heard? Yes verily, their sound went into all the earth, and their words unto the ends of the world.” The preaching of the gospel is that which brings salvation. The earth is full of the gospel of Jesus Christ, from the time of Adam when God promised the seed of a woman. It is already gone throughout the earth, from that time until today. God’s Word is already on this earth, not just in heaven. *Jesus already brought it to pass what we can receive in the New Testament.* God’s Word has already gone throughout all the earth, your mouth is on this earth and your heart is on this earth. When we truly confess Jesus as our Lord with our mouth and truly believe in our heart, that is what saves us, we become citizens of heaven.

We have to be careful of what we hear, I once heard a preacher say, “When the Holy Ghost was given, He came from within; He just rose up from within them on the day of Pentecost.” *Are we going to believe man or the Bible?* Acts 2:2: "And suddenly there came a sound from heaven [who are we going to believe? Luke, who wrote the book of Acts, or what we hear or what is said on TV?] as of a rushing mighty wind . . ." John 15:26: "But when the Comforter is come, whom I will send unto you from the Father . . ." (The Father is in heaven, not on the earth.) He sent the Holy Ghost from heaven, a sound from heaven as a rushing mighty wind (Acts 2:2). It was the coming of the Holy Spirit, to fill the believers.

Jesus had to go to heaven in order to send the Holy Ghost. In John 15:26, He said ". . . when the *Comforter* is come, whom I will send unto you from the Father even the *spirit of truth,* which proceedeth from the Father, he shall testify of me," We know that the word of salvation is on this earth; the word is already out there. Since the time God promised Adam and Eve that the seed would come, the word of faith and has gone forth throughout the entire world. John 16:7: "Nevertheless I tell you the truth; It is expedient for you that I go away: for if I go not away, the Comforter will not come unto you; but if I depart [go back to the Father], I will send him unto you." Before Jesus sent the Holy Ghost, he ascended to heaven. He sat down at the right hand of the Father, and then he sent the Holy Ghost (Acts 2:2). This is when the New Testament church began.

In Matthew 19:19, Jesus said, "Honour thy father and thy mother: and, Thou shalt love thy neighbor as thyself." Verse 20: "The young man saith unto him, All these things have I kept from my youth up: what lack I yet?" This man already had treasures on this earth; he had gold and silver, and was rich. Verse 21: "Jesus said unto him, If thou will be perfect, go and sell that thou hast, and give to the poor, and thou shalt have treasure in heaven . . ." *He was not telling him that he was going to have treasures on this earth, because he already had riches on this earth.* You are going to have rewards in heaven. His money was his god, so what was he going to do, give it all away and *then claim wealth and riches and get it all back?* No! Or was he going to *confess with his mouth to create wealth on this earth?* He already had wealth; Jesus told him he was going to have treasures in heaven. Not on this earth; he already had the wealth on this earth.

The truth is your wealth and your treasures are being stored up in heaven, which is where your rewards are until the judgment of the believer's works (1 Cor. 3:9-15, 2 Cor. 5:10). Your rewards are going to stay there, because you are storing up treasures in heaven. The Bible says it's the love of money that is the root of all evil. We know it's not money itself, but the obsession with money. That is, when a person begins to love it. Jesus said, "For out of the abundance of the heart the mouth speaketh" (Matt. 12:34)

Living a life of holiness, living a life for God with contentment, and not being anxious but being content is of a great gain. 1 Timothy 6:7: "For we brought nothing into this world, and it is certain we can carry nothing out." These earthly possessions will remain here. Verse 8: "And having food and raiment [clothes], let us be therewith content." Verse 9: "But they that will be rich fall into temptation and a snare, and into many foolish and hurtful lusts, which drown men in destruction and perdition." He did not say saved, nor did he say unsaved; he said, they that are rich, anybody. God is warning us! Verse 10: "For the love of money is the root of all evil." Some (saints) covet after money; they have erred from the faith; the world does not have faith.

We have gone from spiritual things to the material things. We no longer focus abundantly on Jesus, but on financial prosperity with Jesus. ". . . They have pierced themselves through with many sorrows" (1 Tim. 6:10). Riches cannot give us joy, but only temporary happiness. Jesus gives us joy in our hearts. 1 Timothy 6:11: "But thou, O man of God, flee these things: and follow after righteousness, godliness, faith, love, patience, meekness" (spiritual). These are the fruit of the Spirit. *Flee these things* that cause people to err.

Don't set your affections on earthly things. He said, flee from them, and follow after righteousness, godliness, faith, love, and patience. 1 Timothy 6:12: "Fight the good fight of faith, *lay hold on eternal life* . . ." (not financial prosperity). Eternal is not earthly, it is spiritual, forever. ". . . Lay hold on eternal life whereunto thou art called . . ." (1 Tim. 6:12). We are called to lay hold on to eternal life, not earthly things. The money on this earth is going to perish. Verse 17: " Charge them that are rich in this world, that they be not highminded, nor trust in uncertain riches, but in the living God, who giveth us richly all things to enjoy."

You trust in God, you put your faith in God. <u>In Truth # 4, I counted this verse as a positive and a negative; I also counted it as a financial blessing.</u> 1 Timothy 6:18: "That they do good, that they be *rich in good works* [that is where our rewards are], ready to distribute, willing to communicate," to be a blessing to others. When we give we are doing a good work, we are laying up treasures in heaven. We are certainly not laying them up here. If you are giving, then how can you be laying up treasures upon this earth? If God wanted us to be millionaires, or to be financially rich on this earth, He would have told us to lay up treasures on this earth and in heaven.

They are being stored up in heaven when we give them away. 1 Timothy 6:19: "Laying up in store for themselves a good foundation against the time to come, that they may lay hold on eternal life." "Time to come" means the future in eternity. He is not speaking about earthly wealth, but <u>eternal life.</u> We are storing rewards up in heaven.

We are going to have to read the Bible without letting someone manipulate our minds. For a long time I was taught this. I believed this without searching the Scriptures for myself. It sounded good. In fact it was something I wanted to hear. If we want to prosper (be made rich), then we should give to God and He is going to make us rich (wealthy). Wrong! We should give to God's work because we love Him without any conditions. God did not promise to make us rich, wealthy, or a millionaire. He did promise to meet our need, and we might have some left over.

James chapter 4, verse 13: "Go to now, ye that say, To day or to morrow <u>we will go into such a city, and continue there a year, and buy and sell, and get gain</u>" (material things). They were going to invest and make a big profit and become rich. We are going to become wealthy and become millionaires. Does this sound familiar today? Verse 15: *"For that ye ought to say, If the Lord will, we shall live, and do this, or that."* In other words, if the Lord will we shall get gain or not. Verse 16: "But now <u>ye rejoice in your boastings:</u> all such rejoicing is evil." Many say that God blessed them, when many times God had nothing to do with it, which is why James warned us.

We are speaking about what we are going to continue doing here on this earth. We are going to buy and to invest. We are going to make a lot of money and become wealthy. We say that we are going to confess it into existence. God is going to make us millionaires, so people go out all fired up with itching ears and begin to seek houses and lands to buy.

Romans 12:6: "Having their gifts differing according to the grace that is given to us . . ." There are special callings on certain people, some are apostles, some are prophets, etc. *Not everyone has the same callings or gifts.* Romans 12:8: ". . . he that giveth, let him do it with simplicity . . ." God has blessed some with an abundance of finances to spread the gospel and to be a blessing to others through giving.

He promised to save everyone who receives Jesus Christ as their Lord and their Savior. However, everyone is not going to get the same reward in heaven. It depends on what you are doing now; you are storing up treasures in heaven. James 4:14: "Whereas ye know not what shall be on the morrow. For what is your life? It is even a vapour, that appeareth for a little time, and then vanisheth away." We will all die soon, so we shouldn't be focusing on the things of this earth. Walking around and speaking about how we are going become rich. Then we rejoice and boast *saying that the Lord gave us all of this.*

God has put certain people in certain ministries to be there, permanently, until the day they die. But you know what? We hear the prosperity message, and then we move to another city and we buy a house for a cheaper price and boast saying, "Look what the Lord has done." Most of the time God has nothing to do with it. Almost anyone can buy a house, even the sinner. Sometimes God is involved, and sometimes He is not. *God places us in a certain ministry for His purpose, plan, and perfect will.* Often we think we are manipulating God; we begin to boast about how great we are doing financially. The Bible says our rejoicing is evil. James is saying that we are rejoicing in our earthly gain.

Colossians 3:1: "If ye then be risen with Christ [God saw us raised up with Christ], seek those things which are above, where Christ sitteth on the right hand of God." Verse 2: "Set your affections on things above . . ." (spiritual things, moral values). This is not a suggestion. The word "affections" here means to think or to set your mind on moral interests, the things above—not on earthly things. It is about a lifestyle of virtue, truth, and spiritual things which are written in 2 Peter 1:5-7. Seek those things, not the things of the earth.

God said He would take care of our need. Matthew 6:32: ". . . for your heavenly Father knoweth that you have *need* of all these things." I used to teach the financial and material prosperity message, too, because that's what I was taught. Then the Holy Spirit began to reveal certain scriptures to me. I know how to repent. I ate humble pie, and God began to bless me with an abundance of scriptures, when I humbled myself. Verse 33: "But seek ye first the kingdom of God and his righteousness and all these things shall be added to you." We reason that if we are seeking first the kingdom of God, then He is telling us we can seek money and things secondly. Wrong!

There is nowhere in the New Testament that God tells us to seek either money or riches. In fact, He told us not to seek the things (riches) of this earth. Jesus said in Matthew 6:32 that the Gentiles (ungodly) seek after these things. Colossians 3:2: "Set your affection on things above, not on the things of this earth." We are not to seek them. God knows we need them. If He takes care of the sparrows and lilies of the field, He will take care of us; we don't have to worry. The Bible tells us to seek the Lord and the things above.

Many Christians explode with excitement, jumping up and down, rejoicing with great joy when they hear the financial prosperity message. I am persuaded that as high as 99 percent-plus of the Christians never become rich, millionaires, or wealthy. Our ears began to itch when we hear about having money (2 Tim. 4:3). I once heard with my own ears a preacher say that telling people to be poor and broke is giving them itching ears. Preaching that people need to be poor and broke will never cause 99 percent plus to have itching ears. Don't even think about it! You are insulting the millions of people who are listening to you. <u>God wants us to be millionaires—this type of preaching will cause people to have itching ears.</u>

Colossians 3:3: "For ye are dead, and your life is hid with Christ in God." We are in Christ, He is our perfection, and He is our righteousness. Verse 4: "When Christ, who is our life, shall appear, then shall ye also appear with him in glory" (the resurrection). Hebrews 10:34: "For ye have compassion of me in my bonds, and took joyfully the spoiling of your goods, knowing in yourselves that ye have in heaven a better and enduring substance" than the earthly goods that they shared with him. When someone tells us to give and that God is going to bless us with a hundredfold now, we are giving with the wrong motive. *We should give to God's work because we love Him.*

Our rewards are in heaven. Read what the author of Hebrews wrote. We will receive our rewards at the believer's judgment in heaven. He said you had compassion on me in prison and you took joyfully the spoiling of your goods (in other words they gave into his ministry). Spoiling means the finances and other things they gave him, all of the goods they gave him; the money, food, shelter, gold, etc.

Ephesians 1:3 and 2:6 say that we are <u>blessed with all spiritual blessings in heavenly places in Christ Jesus.</u> That means our rewards are in heaven, in the spirit realm. We say that, by our confession, we can bring our rewards down to this earth into the physical realm. Wrong! Your works will be rewarded in heaven when Jesus comes for the saints. Revelation 22:12 says, "And, behold, *I come quickly and my reward is with me,* to give every man according as his work shall be."

Your salvation is not in heaven; it is in this earth. The word has already gone out into all the earth. The preachers preach upon this earth. The word of faith goes out, we hear, we receive Jesus when we confess Him as our Lord, and we truly believe (trust Him) in our hearts. We saw this in *Romans chapter 10, that salvation is on this earth, but your rewards are being stored up in heaven.* The Holy Ghost came from heaven (Act 2:2), and He filled the believers and dwells in them. We, the believers, are the temple of God; it is not a physical building. Salvation and the filling of the Holy Spirit are gifts; rewards are not gifts, because you labor for them.

Let's look at Hebrews 10:34 again. The spoiling of their goods was given to the author of Hebrews; *God did not promise riches and wealth on this earth.* He said you yourself know that you have <u>in heaven a better and an enduring substance</u>. The stuff on this earth is not going to endure. Possibly, a thousand years from now, the United States won't exist. All of Bill Gates's money will be gone, even if he becomes a true Christian; it will not endure.

Matthew 5:11: "Blessed are ye when man shall revile you [on this earth] and persecute you, and shall say all manner of evil against you falsely, for my sake." Verse 12: "Rejoice, and be exceeding glad: <u>for great is your reward in heaven</u>: for so persecuted they the prophets which were before you." Your rewards are in heaven. John the Baptist had his head cut off by Herod on this earth. How many houses did he receive? None! John the Baptist will receive his rewards in heaven. Philippians 3:19 says, "Whose end is destruction, whose God is their belly, and whose glory is in their shame, <u>who mind earthly things</u>."

We are not going to stay here; our citizenship is in heaven. Phillippians 3:20: "For our_conversation is in heaven [citizenship—not on this earth]." We are just pilgrims and strangers, we are passing through (1 Pet. 2:11). That is why Abraham looked for a heavenly city, a heavenly country. Read Hebrews 11:10,13, and 16. Abraham possessed the physical land of Israel. That was all he could receive because no one was born again. Spiritually, they were all dead. *Spiritually we are all alive because of what Jesus has done for us;* Jesus said he who is least in the kingdom of God (born again) is greater than John the Baptist, because at that time he was under the Old Testament. <u>When Jesus sent the Holy Spirit, Abraham became born again; he became righteous.</u> Abraham lived under the Old Testament; he was not righteous, but his faith was counted to him for righteousness. Although he was not born again, God counted his faith as righteousness.

When we get into the New Testament, we are made righteous (Rom. 5:19, 2 Cor. 5:21), being justified by faith in Jesus. We have the righteousness of God (Rom. 3:25, 26) because of Jesus. He is our perfection; He is our completion. We (the inner men) are perfect in Jesus. Philippians 3:20: "For our conversation [citizenship] is in heaven, from whence also we look for the Savior, the Lord Jesus Christ." Even though we are on this earth, our citizenship is in heaven.

Last year, we went to Mexico, yet we were still citizens of the United States. We were just visiting Mexico, and were strangers. Our citizenship is in heaven. *If we are sojourning here, why are we running around talking about how rich we can be on this earth?* We are just passing through. Why are we setting our minds and affections on these things? How rich we become on this earth has absolutely nothing to do with our spiritual walk with God—zero!

We should be giving thanks to God for His abundance of grace and His love for us. 2 Corinthians 4:16 says, "For which cause we faint not [we don't give up]; but though our outward man [this body is dying] perish, yet the inward man is renewed day by day." Verse 17: "For our light affliction which is but for a moment, worketh for us a far more exceeding and eternal weight of glory" (spiritual). There is a lot of affliction in this earth that we are going to go through. The persecutions and afflictions are going to bring for us a far more exceeding eternal weight of glory. *We are not going to be weighted down with millions and millions of dollars. We are going to be weighted down with glory—spiritual.* Verse 18: "While we look not at the things which are seen [earthly things, the things that are seen, the financial, material things], but at the things which are not seen for the things which are seen are temporal; but the things which are not seen are eternal."

Heavenly things are eternal, while earthly things are temporary. 2 Corinthians 5:1: "For we know that if our earthly house of this tabernacle were dissolved, we have a building of God, an house not made with hands, eternal in the heavens" (*our new bodies). Our rewards and everything else are in heaven.* Our salvation is upon this earth; we receive it when we confess with our mouth and believe with our heart that Jesus is Lord.

Our reward comes after the judgment in heaven (Rom. 14:10, 1 Cor. 3:13). Second Corinthians 5:10: "For we must all appear before the judgment seat of Christ; that every one may receive the things done in his body, according to that he has done, whether it be good or bad." Our lifestyle and works are going to be rewarded. If they are good, we are going to receive a reward. If they are bad, we will lose that reward. You can read this in 1 Corinthians 3:13, 14, and 15—our works will be tested by fire (fire is a symbol to see if they are good or not). If they pass the test like gold, silver, or precious stones, then we will receive our reward. But if they are like wood, stubble, or hay, then they will burn up, and we will lose our reward. *Not our salvation, our rewards are from our works.*

2 Corinthians 5:11: "Knowing therefore the terror of the Lord [He is going to judge everyone], we persuade men; but we are made manifest unto God; and I trust also are made manifest in your consciences." We are instructing you that, you better live for God because everything is going to be judged. Not your salvation, your total works. He is not going to pick out a certain sin and say, "Yeah, remember that sin." If you don't repent of it now, He will judge it then. <u>The blood of Jesus remits our sins; He will not remember them.</u> In Ephesians 2:10, it says "we are his workmanship created in Christ Jesus unto good works, which God hath before ordained that we should walk in them." *We are going to be rewarded; our works will be judged.*

In Titus 3:5, God says ". . . he saved us, by the washing of regeneration, and renewing of the Holy Ghost" (new birth), which is our salvation. Verse 6 says "Which he shed on us abundantly [salvation—spiritually, not money, not riches, not wealth, but the Holy Ghost] through Jesus Christ our Saviour." Verse 7: "That being justified by his grace, we should be made heirs [Gal. 4:7, and joint heirs with Jesus, as seen in Rom. 8:17] according to the hope of eternal life." Verse 8: "This is a faithful saying, and these things I will that thou affirm constantly, that they which have believed in God might be *careful to maintain good works [because God is going to reward us in* heaven]. These things are good and profitable unto men."

The <u>key</u> point is that Jesus warned us not to lay up treasures on this earth, because these earthly things are temporary. He commanded us to store up treasures in heaven (spiritual things) because they are eternal. In John 6:27, *Jesus said for us not to labor for the things that perish but that which endures unto everlasting life.*

CHAPTER 10

Truth # 9:

Jesus Was Neither Financially Wealthy nor Rich; God Met Jesus' Need, the Same as He Promised to Meet Ours Today

Micah 5:2: ". . . though thou be <u>little</u> among the thousands of Judah, yet out of thee [Bethlehem] shall he come forth unto me that is to be ruler in Israel . . ." I believe God was trying to get a point across to us. If God is God and He is Almighty, why didn't He put Jesus in the Jerusalem Sheraton or in the Bethlehem Hilton (symbolic names)? They couldn't even get a room. The Holy Spirit could have moved on someone to give up their room at the Jerusalem Sheraton, the Bethlehem Hilton, or the best of the inns in those days.

Read the story of the Good Samaritan (Luke 10:30-37). If a certain Samaritan can put a man in an inn and take care of him, <u>why didn't God have Jesus born in the best of the best inns (prosperity messages today)?</u> Acts 11:26: ". . . And the disciples were called Christians first in Antioch." What is a Christian? A Christian is a true follower of Christ, an imitator of Christ. The people of Antioch called them Christians because they saw something in the saints that was in Christ. What was Jesus like? How did Jesus live? *God met Jesus' need; He did not make Jesus financially rich, nor did He make Him wealthy.* In fact, Jesus started off poor; He was born in a stable and <u>not</u> in a five-star hotel or inn.

Luke 2:7: "And she brought forth her firstborn son, and wrapped him in swaddling clothes, and laid him in a manger; because there was no room for them in the inn." He was born in Bethlehem. Jesus had a miraculous birth, a virgin birth, impossible for mankind, yet by the Spirit of God, Mary conceived. God Himself came in the flesh; if He can do this, why wasn't He born in the Jerusalem Sheraton or the Bethlehem Hilton? There was no room for them in the inn. If God can raise the dead, He certainly can provide a suite for Jesus to be born in. He was born in a manger, where animals lived, and <u>it smelled like animals.</u> God was and is trying to tell us something. The King of Kings, the Lord of Glory was *born in a manger* because there was no room for Him. He could have been born in a rich environment if it was God's will; God had the power. *Jesus came into this world a whole lot closer to being poor then being rich;* so don't let anyone try to deceive you about this. Verse 10: "And the angel said unto them, Fear not: for, behold, I bring you good tidings of great joy, which shall be to all people." Luke 2:11: "For unto you is born this day in the city of David a Saviour, which is Christ the Lord." Verse 12: "And this shall be a sign unto you; Ye shall find the babe wrapped in swaddling clothes, lying in a manger." If God had angels speaking and appearing, He definitely could have gotten Jesus a first-class place, <u>unless He had a purpose. </u>

This is the circumcision of Jesus, Luke 2:21: "And *when eight days* were accomplished *for the circumcising* of the child, *his name was called Jesus,* which was so named of the angel before he was conceived in the womb." Verse 22: "And when the days of her purification <u>according to the law of Moses . . .</u>" Mary lived under the Old Testament. Leviticus 12:1: "And the Lord spake unto Moses, saying, speak unto the children of Israel, saying." Verse 2: "If a woman have conceived seed [Mary conceived of the Holy Ghost], and born a man child then she shall be unclean seven days; according to the days of the separation for her infirmity shall she be unclean." Verse 3: "And in the *eighth day* the flesh of his foreskin *shall be circumcised.*" Verse 4: "And *she shall then continue in the blood of her purifying three and thirty days;* she shall touch no hallowed thing, nor come into the sanctuary, until the days of her purifying be fulfilled [a male]."

The four Gospels occurred under the Old Testament, the law of Moses, although they are placed in the New Testament. That is why Mary had to obey the law of Moses. Luke 2:22: "And when the days of her purification according to the law of Moses were accomplished, they brought him to Jerusalem, to present Him to the Lord." Verse 23: "(As it is written in the law of the LORD, Every male that openeth the womb shall be called holy to the Lord;)." Verse 24: "And to offer a sacrifice according to that which is said in the law of the Lord, a pair of turtledoves, or two young pigeons." Leviticus 12:6: "And when the days of her purifying are fulfilled, for a son, or for a daughter, she shall bring a lamb of the first year for a burnt offering, and a young pigeon, or a turtledove, for a sin offering, unto the door of the tabernacle of the congregation, unto the priest." The priest shall make atonement for her, and she shall be clean.

Leviticus 12:8: " And if she be not able to bring a lamb [in other words if you lack the finances, you are too poor, you are not able], then she shall bring two turtles, or two young pigeons . . ." Isn't that what it said in Luke 2:24? Read it. In Luke 2:23: "As it is written in the law of the Lord, Every male that openeth the womb shall be called holy to the Lord." Verse 24: "And to offer a sacrifice according to that which is said in the law of the Lord, A pair of turtle doves, or two young pigeons . . ." Luke did not mention anything about them having brought a lamb. Read what it says in Leviticus 12:8: "And if she be not able to bring a lamb, then she shall bring two turtles, or two young pigeons; the one for the burnt offering, and the other for a sin offering: and the priest shall make atonement for her, and she shall be clean." She didn't bring a lamb, because she was *not* able. *The word "able" in the Hebrew is dahee (enough, sufficient, too much).* Not enough, not sufficient, not too much means to lack.

The Bible said they were supposed to bring a lamb. They lacked a lamb. There were lambs of the first year around, because the shepherds had just visited them. Even God didn't move upon the shepherds to bring a lamb. They always had sacrifices, why didn't they have a lamb around? Maybe God didn't tell the shepherds to bring one. God is sovereign, He does everything His way. The end result is they didn't sacrifice a lamb. There were many animals in Israel, because that is what they offered for sacrifices at the temple. For a male child, they were supposed to bring a lamb of the first year and a pair of turtle doves or two young pigeons. Verse 8: But if you are not able to bring the lamb, you can bring two turtle doves or two pigeons. We need to study the Bible very carefully.

For example, in Matthew chapter 2, the Bible speaks about wise men from the east coming to Jerusalem. I believe there were more than just three wise men, as tradition teaches. There were three types of gifts: gold, frankincense, and myrrh, not three wise men. *A caravan would have had quite a number of people.* There could have been ten wise men; we don't really know. In Luke's Gospel, Jesus was called a *baby;* in Matthew, he was called *a young child.* In Luke, he was in a *manger;* in Matthew, he was in a *house.* Matthew 2:7: "Then Herod, when he had privily called the wise men, enquired of them diligently what time the star appeared." Verse 8: "And he sent them to Bethlehem, and said, Go and search diligently for the young child [not a baby]; and when ye have found him, bring me word again, that I may come and worship him also." Herod really wanted to kill Him. Verse 11: "And when they were come into the house."

In Luke, it said a manger. This is a house, He is somewhat older, and that is why Herod killed all the male children two and under. Luke 2:11: ". . . they saw the young child with Mary his mother [Matthew's Gospel said nothing about Joseph being there; maybe he was out working. However, when you get to Luke's Gospel, it speaks about both of them being there.], and fell down, and worshipped him: and when they had opened their treasures, they presented unto him gifts; gold, and frankincense and myrrh." Three wise men are not in the Bible. That is religious tradition of men. In Mark 7:13, *Jesus warned us about making the Word of God, the Bible, "of none effect" through our traditions.*

We read in 2 Timothy 3:16 that all Scripture is given for doctrine, for reproof, for correction, and for instruction. It is not a manger; it is not a stable, but a house. It didn't say a baby. Maybe, He has grown somewhat, 4 to 8 months, who knows? *We really don't know.* In those days, they traveled by caravan, they came all the way from the east, possibly as far as Persia, where they first saw the star. Three wise men, who are rich, are not likely to travel by themselves from the Far East with a lot of money.

In Matthew 2:13: "And when they were departed, behold, the angel of the Lord appeareth to Joseph in a dream, saying, Arise, and take the <u>young child</u> and his mother, and flee into Egypt and be thou there until I bring thee word: for Herod will seek the young child to destroy him." Verse 14: "When he arose he took the young child and his mother by night, and departed into Egypt." He did not linger around for a week preparing and getting their things together. They left immediately! I believe that is why the gold, frankincense, and myrrh were given to them by God to take care of them until they became established in Egypt. When Jesus was born, they didn't have much. They couldn't afford to buy a lamb at that time, or they disobeyed the law of Moses, Leviticus 12:6, which said, ". . . <u>she</u> <u>shall</u> bring a lamb of the first year . . . and a young pigeon, or a turtledove . . ."

Was Joseph a cheapskate? If the wise men were there at the manger, they would have the gold, frankincense, and myrrh. DO we believe that Joseph kept the gold, etc, and, being cheap, bought just two turtledoves or two young pigeons, hoping that God won't know? Saying, "We won't buy a lamb—that costs too much." <u>No!</u> <u>No! No!</u> I believe they did not have the funds to buy a lamb of the first year, since they didn't sacrifice one. According to the time from the birth of Jesus, to the circumcision (eight days), to the purification of Mary (thirty-three days, a male) to be fulfilled, there was a total of forty-one days before she would have offered up the lamb in the temple. They still could have bought a lamb of the first year.

Matthew 6:11: "Give us this day <u>our daily bread</u>." *Why didn't Jesus pray to make us wealthy or rich?* Daily means to have our need met each and every day. Matthew 11:7: "And as they departed, Jesus began to say unto the multitudes concerning John, What went ye out into the wilderness to see? A reed shaken with the wind?" The answer is no. Verse 8: "But what went ye out for to see? A man clothed in *soft raiment? Behold, they that wear soft clothing are in kings' houses.*" Jesus was asking them if they went to see a man that was rich, and very prosperous in expensive clothes. Verse 9: "But what went ye out for to see? A prophet? yea, I say unto you and more than a prophet." Verse 11: "Verily I say unto you, among them that are <u>born of women there hath not risen a greater than John the Baptist</u>: notwithstanding <u>he that is least in the kingdom of heaven is greater</u> than he." *The least saint today is greater than John was in his day, because of the blood of Jesus.* The Bible said that *John wore camel's skin, not soft clothing.*

Matthew 17:24: "And when they were come to Capernaum, they that received tribute money came to Peter, and said, Doth not your master pay tribute?"(taxes). Verse 25: "He saith, Yes. And when he was come into the house, Jesus prevented him, saying, What thinkest thou, Simon? Of whom do the kings of the earth take custom or tribute? of their own children or of strangers?" <u>"Prevented" means Jesus spoke to Peter first;</u> it didn't mean that He kept Peter from entering the house. Verse 26: "Peter saith unto him, Of strangers. Jesus saith unto him, Then are the children free." Verse 27: "Notwithstanding, lest we should offend them, go thou to the sea, and cast an hook, and take up the fish that first cometh up; and when thou hast opened his mouth, thou shalt find a piece of money: that take, and give unto them <u>for me</u> and <u>thee</u>." If He had an abundance of money all the time, why didn't He just take it out of the treasure or out of the house? Why did Jesus tell Peter to go catch a fish in order to pay their taxes? I believe they didn't have any money on them at the time. He had a reason for everything He said and everything He did. When Jesus said this, it was God revealing to Him the money inside of the fish. He didn't say to go into the other room and take the money out of the treasure.

There were times when they didn't have enough money, they lacked (abased). In John 6:7, *Philip* said that their finances were not were sufficient to buy enough bread. *Paul* (2 Cor. 11:27) lacked at times, so did *Peter and John* (Acts 3:6). Now, *Jesus* didn't have any money, and He sent Peter to catch a fish. God met His need; it was just enough money to pay their taxes. God always met His need, and He also promised to meet all our need. He didn't tell Peter to jump into the water, swim to the bottom, and you will find a lost treasure full of gold. Then He could tell everyone that they were rich, saying the <u>Father wanted them to be wealthy (itching ears).</u> God could have done that, but He didn't. God met His need.

The Gospel of Luke, chapter 8, verse 1: "And it came to pass afterward, that he went throughout every city and village, preaching, and shewing the glad tidings of the kingdom of God: and the twelve were with him" (apostles). Verse 2: "And certain women, which had been healed of evil spirits and infirmities, Mary called Magdalene, out of whom went seven devils" (seven evil spirits cast out of Mary Magdalene). Verse 3: "And Joanna the wife of Chuza, Herod's steward, and Susanna, and many others, which <u>ministered unto him of their substance</u>." God again met Jesus' need through their substance. They ministered unto Him with their food, clothes, homes, etc. *Jesus did not say that God would make them rich or wealthy.* Jesus Himself was neither rich nor wealthy. God met His need through others. *Jesus was neither a millionaire nor did He have a very rich bank account.*

Matthew, chapter 21, verse 1 says, "And when they drew nigh unto Jerusalem, and were come to Bethphage, unto the mount of Olives, then sent Jesus two disciples." Verse 2: "Saying unto them, Go into the village over against you, and straightway ye shall find an ass tied, and a colt with her: loose them, and bring them unto me." Verse 3: "And if any man say ought unto you, ye shall say, The <u>Lord hath *need*</u> of them; and straightway he will send them." God shall supply all our need. He had a need, God supplied His need. God had already spoken to the men's hearts. God speaks to people's hearts to meet our need.

John 12:1: "Then Jesus six days before the passover came to Bethany, where Lazarus was which had been dead, whom he raised from the dead." Verse 2: "There <u>they made him a supper</u> [God was meeting His need through them]; and Martha served: but Lazarus was one of them that sat at the table with him." Verse 3: "Then took Mary a pound of ointment of spikenard, very costly, and anointed the feet of Jesus, and wiped his feet with her hair; and the house was filled with the odour of the ointment." Judas Iscariot complained to her about wasting the ointment. Verse 7: "Then said Jesus, Let her alone: against the day of my burying hath she kept this." Even through <u>the anointing for His burial, God, through Mary,</u> met His need.

In Mark 14:13-15, Jesus told two of His disciples to find and follow a certain man with a pitcher of water. He was going to go into a house with a large upper room furnished. God had already prepared a place for them to eat the Passover.

John's Gospel, chapter 19, verse 1 says, "Then Pilate therefore took Jesus, and scourged him." Verse 2: "And the soldiers platted a crown of thorns, and put it on his head, and <u>they put on him a purple robe.</u>" Verse 3: "And said, Hail, King of the Jews! . . ." (they mocked him). It's *their robe* of royalty. Matthew 27:30: "And they spit upon him, and took the reed and smote him on the head." Verse 31: "And after that they had mocked him, they took the robe off from him, and put his own raiment on him, and led him away to crucify him." Verse 32: "And as they came out, they found a man of Cyrene, Simon by name: and him they compelled to bear his cross." God supplied someone to help Him; He didn't give Him twenty people, but He supplied one. God moved upon the Romans when He couldn't bear the cross anymore. God met His need.

John 19:17 "And he bearing his cross, went forth to a place called the place of a skull . . ." The crown of thorns, the purple robe, and the cross were *all provided by the Romans, nothing of His.* God met His need, so that He could die for us. Verse 19: "And Pilate wrote a title [Jesus did not write the title, God is moving upon Pilate to write this because the Jews didn't want this written], and put it on the cross. And the writing was JESUS OF NAZARETH THE KING OF THE JEWS." Verse 20: "This title then read many of the Jews: for the place where Jesus was crucified was nigh to the city: and it was written in <u>Hebrew,</u> and <u>Greek</u> and <u>Latin.</u> *There were three inscriptions on the cross.* The chief priest complained to Pilate about what was written. Verse 22: "Pilate answered, What I have written I have written." God had Pilate write this, stating that <u>Jesus is King of the Jews.</u>

Mark 16:1: "And when the sabbath was past, Mary Magdalene and Mary the mother of James, and Salome, had bought sweet spices, that they might come and anoint him." <u>They brought the spices</u> for His body, so that they could anoint His body, because they thought He was still in the tomb. Those weren't His spices that they were bringing, but theirs. God met Jesus' burial need.

Joseph was the man God had prepared to remove the body from the cross and to bury Him. Verse 38: "And after this Joseph of Arimathaea, being a disciple of Jesus, but secretly for fear of the Jews, besought Pilate that he might take away the body of Jesus: and Pilate gave him leave. He came therefore, and took the body of Jesus." Verse 39: "And there came also Nicodemus, which at the first came to Jesus by night, and brought a mixture of myrrh and aloes, about an hundred pound weight." Verse 40: "Then took they the body of Jesus, and wound it in linen clothes with the spices . . ." (the spices of Nicodemus). Everything Jesus received was God meeting His need *through someone else*. God did not give Him hundreds and thousands of anything. He gave Him exactly what He needed. How many linen clothes did they need to wrap the body? Let's say, one or two, and that's what He received. How many tombs did He need? He received one tomb. God met His need. Jesus was buried in a tomb provided by Joseph of Arimathaea. God met His need; He didn't receive hundreds or thousands; *God gave him exactly what He needed.*

In Acts 3:1, it says, "Now Peter and John went up together into the temple at the house of prayer, being the ninth hour" (that's 3 PM, Jewish time, not Western time). Verse 2: "And a certain man lame from his mother's womb was carried, whom they laid daily at the gate of the temple which is called Beautiful, to ask alms of them that entered into the temple." He is asking alms, when people ask for *alms* they are asking for *money or goods*. Verse 4: "And Peter, fastening his eyes upon him with John, said, Look on us." Verse 5: "And he gave heed unto them expecting to receive something of them." Verse 6: "Then Peter said, Silver and gold have I none . . ." *We don't have any money; today many would call that a bad confession.* We don't hear anyone preaching that today. At that present time they did not have any money, neither Peter nor John. "Silver and gold have I none." The apostles Peter and John said that they didn't have any money. Verse 6: ". . . but such as I have I give thee: In the name of Jesus Christ of Nazareth rise up and walk." Peter lifted the man, and the man was healed.

"And the multitude of them that believed were of one heart and of one soul; neither said any of them that ought of the things which he possessed was his own; but they had all things common"(Acts 4:32). Acts 4:33: "And with great power gave the apostles witness of the resurrection of the Lord Jesus: and great grace was upon them all." Verse 34: "Neither was there any among them that lacked . . ." Their need was met and they lacked nothing; he did not make anyone rich. "For as many as were possessors of lands or houses sold them and brought the prices of the things that were sold."

The wealthy and rich were selling their stuff and giving it to the people who lacked. They were not building big mansions and possessing five homes worth a million dollars each. They knew that in heaven they were storing up great rewards for eternity. Acts 4:34: ". . . for as many as were possessors of lands or houses sold them . . ." We are not even close to that; today many are trying to possess houses and lands. Verse 35: "And laid them down at the apostles' feet: and distribution was made unto every man according as he had need." My God shall supply all your need. He didn't make anyone rich.

Paul says in 2 Corinthians 11:21, "I speak as concerning reproach, as though we had been weak. Howbeit whereinsoever any is bold, (I speak foolishly,) [I am going to speak as a fool; I am going to brag on myself is what he was saying, so that he could get his point across.] I am bold also." Verse 22: "Are they Hebrews? so am I. Are they Israelites? so am I. Are they the seed of Abraham? so am I." They don't have anything that I don't have. Verse 23: "Are they ministers of Christ? (I speak as a fool) I am more [When you boast about yourself, you are a fool in the eyes of God.]; in labours more abundant, in stripes above measure, in prisons more frequent, in deaths oft." Verse 24: "Of the Jews five times received I forty stripes save one" (I was beaten five times with thirty-nine stripes). Verse 25: "Thrice was I beaten with rods, once was I stoned, thrice I suffered shipwreck, a night and a day I have been in the deep" (24 hours in the sea,). Verse 26: "In journeyings often, in perils of waters, in perils of robbers, in perils by mine own countrymen, in perils by the heathen, in perils in the city, in perils in the wilderness, in perils in the sea, in perils among false brethren," Verse 27: "In weariness and painfulness, in watchings often, in hunger and thirst . . ."

This is a true Christian life, suffering for Jesus. There are times that the saints in Afghanistan, Iraq, and many other places lack food. They have left the luxuries of life, houses, cars, and all of the material things of this world to serve Jesus. We who are in America are living a prosperous life while they are lacking many of the basic things of life. They will be rewarded at the believers' judgment. Jesus said that "many that are first [*we think*] shall be last; and the last [*we think*] shall be first" (Matt. 19:30).

In hunger and thirst, someone might say that Paul was fasting. No! He said, "in fasting often" (2 Cor. 11:27). Fasting is voluntary, hunger and thirst are involuntary. If a person doesn't have anything, then he is not fasting, he is broke. Philippians 4:12: "I know both how to be abased, and I know how to abound; every where and in all things I am instructed both to be full and to be hungry . . ." He knew how to be hungry (2 Cor. 11:27).

The <u>key</u> point is that Jesus was born in a manger and not in a mansion. There was a reason why He was born in a manger with the sheep and the cattle. <u>He was buried in a tomb that belonged to someone else, Joseph of Arimathea.</u> The Bible said that "*he became poor,* that ye through his poverty might *be rich*" (2 Cor. 8:9, *spiritually rich,* many were already materially and financially rich) with salvation, relationship with God, indwelling of the Spirit, fruit of the Spirit, joint heirs with Jesus, heirs of the Father etc.

CHAPTER 11

Truth # 10:

Presumptuous, Jesus
Owned a Large House

Presume means to take for granted, to assume to be true. People presume things that are not in the Bible. They presume it because that's what they want to believe and so they just accept it. They presume that <u>Jesus had a large house in Capernaum</u>. I have heard this preached. Matthew 8:19: "And a certain scribe came, and said unto him, Master, I will follow thee wherever thou goest." Verse 20: "And Jesus said unto him the foxes have holes, and the birds of the air have nests; but the Son of man hath not where to lay his head."

A hole to a fox is its house and a place of security where it raises its family. *The bird's nest is its house,* a place of security where it raises its family. Jesus said foxes have holes and birds have nests, but the *Son of man does not have anywhere to lay his head; He didn't own a house*. Nests and holes are physical buildings. Although they may be a hole in the earth (foxes' buildings) and a nest in a tree (birds' building), these are their houses. Jesus was comparing the foxes' holes and the birds' nests, which they have, with His lack of a house.

We are going to see how Scriptures are misinterpreted. He did not have a place to lay His head in <u>His own house.</u> God met His need and provided Him a place to stay. Jesus said the Son of Man (Jesus) has nowhere to lay His head. Does that mean He didn't sleep? Certainly, He slept! He used the foxes' holes and birds' nests as a metaphor, referring to their houses where they dwell. They dwell there, not just sleep there, like in a hotel or in an inn. This was their main dwelling place; Jesus said the Son of Man didn't have a house, a place to lay His head.

In John's Gospel, chapter 1, beginning with verse 37, it says that two of His disciples heard Jesus speak, and they followed Him. Jesus turned, and saw them following and said unto them, "What seek ye?" They said unto him "Master, where dwellest thou?" Verse 39: "He saith unto them Come, and see. They came and saw where He dwelt and abode with him <u>that day . . .</u>"

John 1:26 "John answered them, saying, I baptize with water: but there standeth one among you, whom ye know not." Verse 27: "He it is, who coming after me is preferred before me, whose shoe's latchet I am not worthy to unloose." Verse 28: "These things were done in Bethabara beyond Jordan, where John was baptizing." This was where John was operating and baptizing the people. Jesus did not have a house in that area; in fact, He came there to be baptized by John. *During this time, Jesus lived in Nazareth.* Bethabara is near Jerusalem; He said to come and see where He dwelled. <u>He did not mean for them to go from Bethabara to Nazareth, which is over sixty miles.</u> He said, "Come and see" where He dwelled. Did that mean He wanted them to go all the way to Nazareth?

We presume that He had a house in Nazareth because He was a carpenter. Joseph also dwelled in Nazareth; Jesus was a young man and He lived with his father and mother. Since Joseph was a carpenter, he was the one who most likely built the house where they lived. But wait a minute; He's not in Nazareth but in Bethabara, which is located near the southern end of the Jordan River. They came and saw where He dwelled. *Do you believe that they walked sixty-plus miles to see where He dwelt?* I don't think so. And they "abode with Him that day for it was about the tenth hour" (John 1:39).

When He said where He dwelled, are we presuming that He had a house in Bethabara? No! He could have been sleeping in the garden, renting a room in an inn, or living with friends. He's not going to travel all the way to Nazareth sixty-plus miles away; *it is already about 4 PM.* John 1:39: ". . . They came and saw where he dwelt and abode with him that day: for it was about the tenth hour." You try walking sixty miles after 4 PM and see if you get there that day. Mark 1:5 says, He was in the land of Judea, which is in the southern part of Israel.

This presumptuous teaching comes from the words *"the house."* You will see this a number of times in the Bible. We presume that it was a large house that Jesus owned. *There are many scriptures where the word "house" is used, and it doesn't mean it is Jesus' house.* The house is in relationship to whatever house a person is speaking of. Let us say that I was painting a certain person's house; I went outside and had lunch. If I said that I went back into "the house," then it is not my house; it is the house I am painting.

Mark 2:1: "And again he entered into Capernaum after some days; and it was noised [that means it was the general belief] that he was in the house." We are going to see that it is not Jesus' house; it was someone else's house. Verse 2: "And straightway many were gathered together, insomuch that there was no room to receive them, no, not so much as about the door [We see there were so many people and we assume that He had a big house which He owned.]: and he preached the word unto them." Verse 3: "And they came unto him, bringing one sick of the palsy, which was borne of four." Jesus did a lot of ministering in Capernaum, and I believe He moved to Capernaum and dwelled there (Matthew 4:13). Verse 4: "And when they could not come nigh unto him for the press, they uncovered the roof where he was: and when they had broken it up, they let down the bed in which the sick of the palsy lay." Verse 5: "When Jesus saw their faith, he said unto the sick of the palsy, Son, thy sins be forgiven thee." Verse 6: "But there were certain of the scribes sitting there, and reasoning in their hearts." Verse 7: "Why doth this man thus speak blasphemies? who can forgive sins but God only?" Jesus told the man that his sins were forgiven him and to take up his bed and go his way into the house. Verse 12 says that immediately the man arose, took up his bed, and went to his house. *The house in verse 1 many would say was Jesus' house in Capernaum; that's presumptuous.* Do I believe Jesus owned a house? I don't know, but I'm not going to presume it: I know <u>one fact</u> is that <u>Jesus said that the Son of man has nowhere to lay his head</u>. *Do we believe that He was lying, or was He telling the truth?*

Another point is in Mark 6:1: "And he went out from thence, and came into his own country; and his disciples follow him." Verse 3: "Is not this the carpenter, the son of Mary, the brother of James, and Joses, and of Juda, and Simon? and are not his sisters *here* with us? And they were offended at him." Verse 4: "But Jesus, said unto them, A prophet is not without honour, but in his own country, and among his own kin, and in <u>his own house.</u>" Luke 4:16 says, "And he came to Nazareth, where He had been brought up . . ." He grew up there. He no longer lived in Nazareth, *yet He stated in Mark 6:4 that it was His own house.* Some presume that this is His house; it probably was Mary, His mother's, house, which Joseph His father had built, where Jesus was raised. *Mark 6:3 did mention that Mary and her children lived there.* <u>Yet, Jesus refers to this as His own house.</u>

The Scriptures say in Matthew 8:15 and Luke 4:38 that He went *into Peter's house* and He healed Peter's mother in-law. Mark 1:29 said it was Peter's and Andrew's house, not just Peter's house. The mother-in-law was also living with them. We have to divide the Word of God rightly: if we took Matthew 8:15 by itself, it would be Peter' house alone.

When they said in His own country, did He own the country? No! He's a citizen of that country. If someone told me to go back to my own country, I don't own the country, I am a citizen of this country, the United States of America. I don't own it; if I did I would be the richest man in the world. I'm a citizen of this nation, there is a relationship. The Bible says His own kin; did He own them, His mother, His brothers, His sisters? No! He was a part of that family, that's His family, His own house; it means He was a part of that household. All citizens are a part of our country. Insofar as our kin, we are a part of them, but we don't physically own them. We are a part of that family. *The words "in his own house" in Mark 6:4 means His household (family).*

Acts 10:1: "There was a certain man in Caesarea called Cornelius, a centurion of the band called the Italian band." Verse 2: "A devout man, and one that feared God with all his house . . ." We know this is not speaking about a physical house, but about his household, as in Mark 6:4. Jesus said, "the Son of man hath not where to lay his head" (Matt. 8:20). *He was not speaking about not having a place to sleep,* because He said foxes have holes and birds have nests, and those are their houses.

Acts chapter 16, verse 23 says Paul and Silas were thrown into jail, and in verse 26, it says "a great earthquake" came and all the people were freed. Verse 25: "And at midnight Paul and Silas prayed, and sang praises unto God and the prisoners heard them." Verse 26: "And suddenly there was a great earthquake, so that the foundations of the prison were shaken; and immediately all the doors were opened, and everyone's bands were loosed." Verse 27: "And the keeper of the prison, awaking out of his sleep, and seeing the prison doors open, he drew out his sword, and would have killed himself, supposing that the prisoners had been fled." Verse 28: "But Paul cried with a loud voice saying, Do thyself no harm: for we are all here." The jailer fell down before Paul and Silas. Verse 30: "And brought them out, and said, Sirs, what must I do to be saved?" Verse 31: "And they said, Believe on the Lord Jesus Christ, and thou shalt be saved, and thy house." Do we believe He was speaking about a physical building? No! He was speaking about people, not about a physical building. They were not talking about the keeper of the prison's house; they were speaking about a relationship. So when Jesus spoke about *"in his own house" in Mark 6:4,* He spoke the same thing as in Acts 16:31.

Again, we have to study so that we can rightly divide the Word of truth (2 Timothy 2:15). Matthew 17:24 says, "And when they were come to Capernaum, they that received tribute money came to Peter, and said, Doth not your master pay tribute?" Verse 25: "He saith, Yes. And when he was come into the house, Jesus prevented him [The word prevented means He spoke to Peter first, before Peter could say anything.], saying, What thinkest thou, Simon? of whom do the kings of the earth take custom or tribute? of their own children, or of strangers?" Verse 26: "Peter saith unto Him, Of strangers. Jesus saith unto him, Then are the children free."

Then, He sent Peter to catch a fish that had money in its mouth. He told Peter to give it to the tax collectors for Himself and Peter. In Matthew 17:25, it said, ". . . when he was come into the house . . ." There's that word "house," so some say that Jesus had a house and He had to pay taxes, but Peter is also paying tax. We know Peter did not live with Jesus, because, in Mark 1:29,30, Peter lived with his wife and Andrew. Now there are other scriptures where the words "the house" are written (Matt. 9:28, 13:1,36, and Mark 9:33).

In Matthew chapter 2, verse 10, we are going to see *that the house is neither Jesus nor Joseph's house.* The wise men came from the east, and when they saw the star, they rejoiced with exceedingly great joy. Verse 11: "And when they were come into the house . . ." Now wait a minute, that's not Joseph's house; he didn't own the house there; he came down because of the registration. He left Nazareth to go down to Bethlehem to be registered because of the decree from Caesar Augustus. Joseph did not move to Bethlehem to live or stay; He lived in Nazareth. Jesus grew up in Nazareth, which is why He is called Jesus of Nazareth. When the wise men came into the house, what house? *The house where Joseph and Mary were staying, possibly renting.* Again, Joseph did not own the house.

When the wise men came in, they saw a young child, and began to worship Him. They gave Him three different types of gifts: gold, frankincense, and myrrh. *The Bible mentions nothing about three wise men.* However, it does mention three types of gifts, not three wise men. This is not scriptural. Matthew 2:13: "And when they were departed, behold, the angel of the Lord appeareth to Joseph in a dream, saying, Arise, and take the young child and his mother, and flee into Egypt . . ." An angel appeared to Joseph and told him to leave because Herod was trying to kill Jesus and all the firstborn sons. Verse 14: "When he arose," that meant he left immediately into Egypt. If that was Joseph's house, he would have had to sell it, which would have delayed him. Now, if he was renting from someone, he would pay the daily or weekly rent like we do at a motel, and he would be able to leave that night without any problems.

Matthew 9:9: "And as Jesus passed forth from thence, he saw a man, named Matthew, sitting at the receipt of custom: and he saith unto him, Follow me. And he arose, and followed him." Verse 10: "And it came to pass, as Jesus sat at meat in the house, behold, many publicans and sinners came and sat down with him and his disciples." Verse 11: "And when the Pharisees saw it, they said unto his disciples, Why eateth your Master with publicans and sinners?" We could presume that the words "the house" refers to Jesus owning it, as some believe, concerning Capernaum.

In Luke 5:29, it said that Levi (Matthew) made him a great feast in whose house? *Matthew made him a great feast in his own house,* and there was a great company of tax collectors and of others who sat down with them. This house in Capernaum wasn't Jesus' house, so when they said "the house," it belonged to Matthew. When you see the words "the house" in Matthew 9:10, *that was not Jesus' house, because when you read the gospel of Luke, you see that it was Matthew's house.* That's the error we make in Mark 2:1 — being presumptuous.

Luke's Gospel, chapter 7, verse 1: "And when he had ended all his sayings in the audience of the people, he entered into Capernaum." Verse 2: "And a certain centurion's servant, who was dear unto him, was sick, and ready to die." He pleaded with Jesus to come and heal his servant. Verse 6: "Then Jesus went with them, and when he was now not far from the house . . ." Whose house? The centurion's house! When we read that Jesus was in the house in Capernaum (Mark 2:1), many presume that it was Jesus' house. The centurion's house was also there in Capernaum and was referred to as the house. No, the house in Mark 2:1 referred to *the house where the roof tile was removed.*

We don't know if it was Jesus' house; *some presume that because they want to make the point that Jesus owned a large house.* Back to Luke 7:6: ". . . And when he was now not far from the house, the centurion sent friends to him, saying unto him, Lord, trouble not thyself: for I am not worthy that thou shouldest enter under my roof." Luke 7:10 says, "And they that were sent, returning to the house, found the servant whole that had been sick." This was the centurion's house, not Jesus' house.

Presumption is when we don't know whose house it was, and we assume whose it was. The house is related to whatsoever is occurring at that time. For example, the words "the house" would be the house where Joseph had the dream, the house where Matthew had a feast and invited the sinners, the house where the centurion's servant who was sick was healed, or in some cases, the Bible doesn't tell us whose house it was, nor does it have to be Jesus' house. We assume that Jesus owned the house because of the words "the house"; we believe He had a large house. Remember, it wasn't just Jesus paying the taxes, so did Peter.

Luke 7:36 says it is the Pharisee's house. Verse 36: "And one of the Pharisees desired him that he would eat with him. And he went into the Pharisee's house, and sat down to meat." *In this case, the Bible tells us who owns the house, but sometimes it does not tell us.* We have to find this out by truly studying the Scriptures, like we found about the centurion's house. So to assume it was Jesus' house is presumptuous. There is nothing in the Bible that tells us that it was truly Jesus' house. But there is one fact that was definitely stated in Matthew 8:20: ". . . the Son of man hath not where to lay his head."

So the Bible says in Luke 7:37,38 that Jesus went down to the Pharisee's house, and a woman in the city, who was a sinner, though she knew that Jesus was eating in the Pharisee's house, brought an alabaster box of ointment and she ministered to Him. The Bible says it was the Pharisee's house. Luke's Gospel chapter 14 speaks about another Pharisee's house, "the house"; remember those words. Luke 14:1: "And it came to pass, as he went into the house . . ." Here the Bible gives us more detail. If we did not have the rest of that verse, presumptuously we would say that this was Jesus' own house. He went into the house of one of the chief Pharisees to eat bread on the Sabbath day, and they watched Him. Now we know the house didn't belong to Jesus; it belonged to one of the chief Pharisees.

Let's go to Luke 8:51: "And when he came into the house, he suffered no man to go in, save Peter and James, and John, and the father and the mother of the maiden." We know the house in this case belonged to Jairus, because verse 41 said the man fell at Jesus' feet and besought Him that He would come into his house.

124

In John chapter 11, we read a story about Martha and Mary, the two sisters, and Lazarus their brother, who died. They were in Bethany, near Jerusalem. Verse 19: "And many of the Jews came to Martha and Mary, to comfort them concerning their brother." Verse 20: "Then Martha, as soon as she heard that Jesus was coming, went and met him: but Mary sat still in the house." There's that phrase again "the house," but whose house? *Mary and Martha's—not Jesus' house.* Jesus then told them about His resurrection. Verse 30: "Now Jesus was not yet come into the town, but was in that place where Martha met him." Verse 31: "The Jews then, which were with her in the house, and comforted her, when they saw Mary, that she rose up hastily and went out, followed her, saying, she goeth unto the grave to weep there."

In Mark 2:4, we are being presumptuous when we say that the house where they uncovered the roof was Jesus' house; it could have been anyone's house. When Jesus was working miracles and healing people, no one was going to be overly concerned about a roof being taken apart. The owner of the house was so excited, he was not going to stand and argue about a roof. He probably said, "Come on in; take the whole roof apart if necessary." *The owner was looking at Jesus, waiting to hear what He was going to say and do.* Verse 5: "When Jesus saw their faith, he said to the sick of the palsy, Son, thy sins be forgiven thee." The man picked up his bed and walked right out and went to his own house. He was full of joy! The owner of the house was full of joy, and so was everyone else there. *Do we believe that they were concerned about a roof?* The Bible doesn't say it was Jesus' house; there again, that is being presumptuous.

Acts 2:1: "And when the day of Pentecost was fully come, they were all with one accord in one place." Verse 2: "And suddenly there came a sound from heaven as of a rushing mighty wind, and it filled all the house where they were sitting." Was this Jesus' house? No! It was the upper room; some say it was Mary's, the mother of Mark's, house. The house here refers to the house where they were all filled with the Holy Ghost in the upper room; *it relates to no other house.* When Jesus said, "I am the way, the truth, and the life" (John 14:6), it relates to Him being the only way, the only truth, and the only eternal life. Acts 2:2 relates to the only place where the 120 disciples were filled with the Holy Ghost on the day of Pentecost. That's the relationship here between *the house and the filling of the Holy Ghost and has nothing to do with who owns it*. The words *"the house,"* that some claim was Jesus' house, *refer only to the house where they removed the tiles and let the man down, who was healed*.

Don't just believe anything—study the Scriptures in detail. Acts 9:11-13 is about Saul (Paul) on his way to Damascus, Syria. Jesus appeared to Ananias, a certain disciple, and told him to go to the street, called Straight, which is in Damascus, Syria, and inquire in the house of Judas for one called Saul of Tarsus, who was praying and had seen in a vision a man, named Ananias, coming in and putting his hand on him so that Paul might receive his sight. Ananias told the Lord that he had heard by many of this man, how much evil he had done to his saints at Jerusalem. Verse 17: "And Ananias went his way and entered into <u>the house . . .</u>" The house of Judas in verse 11, where Saul was praying; *the house that relates to where Saul was at that time was Judas' house*. Verse 17: ". . . Brother Saul, the Lord, even Jesus, that appeared unto thee in the way as thou camest, hath sent me, that thou mightest receive thy sight, and be filled with the Holy Ghost." Saul received salvation on the road to Damascus, when he called Jesus Lord. In other words, what do you want me to do? I surrender!

In Acts 11:11, Peter was in <u>the house</u>—Simon's, a tanner of Joppa by the seaside (Acts 10:6), that's whose house. In Hebrews, chapter 3, verse 2, it says that Moses was faithful to all in his house; he's not speaking about a physical building, as the Bible says we are the house of God.

The <u>key</u> point is that Jesus said, "The foxes have holes, and the birds of the air have nests; but the Son of man hath not where to lay his head" (Matt. 8:20). The Bible doesn't ever reveal that Jesus owned a house that He lived in permanently; however, some assume that He did. <u>The words "the house" sometimes refer to people, sometimes a physical building, and sometimes to other things.</u> *They always relate to the present story.* You have to read that particular story and search it in detail with an open mind to see whether it is true (Acts 17:11).

CHAPTER 12

Truth # 11:

The Blessing of Abraham Is That the Jews and the Gentiles Can Receive the Promise of the Spirit (Holy Spirit to Dwell in Us)

Genesis 12:1: "Now the LORD had said unto Abram [Abraham], Get thee out of thy country, and from thy kindred, and from thy father's house, unto a land that I will shew thee." Verse 2: "And I will make of thee a great nation, and I will bless thee: and make thy name great; and thou shall be a blessing." Verse 3: "And I will bless them that bless thee, and curse him that curseth thee: and in thee shall all families [Gentiles] of the earth be blessed." *The land of Canaan is where Israel is today.* Verse 7: "And the LORD appeared unto Abram, and said, Unto thy seed will I give this land: and there builded he an altar unto the LORD, who appeared unto him."

There are four areas where God made promises to Abraham. The *first* area was *personal promises* God made to Abraham and for him only, neither for Israel, nor for the body of Christ—the church. In Genesis 12:2, God said "I will bless thee, and make thy name great"; these were personal promises to Abraham. I will <u>bless Abraham</u> and <u>make Abraham's name great.</u>

The *second* area was promises *God made to Israel,* the descendent of Abraham according to the flesh. "I will make of thee a great nation" (Israel). In Genesis 15:18, God gave the land to Israel, Abraham's physical seed, "from the river of Egypt [this is not the Nile River] unto the great river, the river Euphrates." There are certain promises He made to Israel in the Old Testament that still exist. One is that the twelve apostles are going to sit on the twelve thrones and judge the twelve tribes of Israel. We are not going to judge Israel. These promises did not pertain to the church. <u>We are the body of Christ, not spiritual Israel</u>. That is unscriptural.

The *third* area of the promise pertains to the *spiritual body of Christ, the true church, where there is neither Jew nor Gentile.* If you are born of the Spirit (John 3:6), then you are a member of the church. We claim the blessings of Abraham, saying that we are the head and not the tail; I am above and not beneath. We are neither the head nor the tail, we are in Christ; <u>Jesus is the head and we are the body!</u> These were the promises God made to Israel (Deut. 28:13) under the law of Moses, not to Abraham; *we are not under the law for blessing nor for cursing.* The blessing of Abraham that God spoke about for us came through Jesus, the seed, and it had nothing to do with us having either riches or material things. These are not the blessing of Abraham.

The true blessing of Abraham was spiritual, that God would dwell in us by His Spirit. This is the <u>promise of the Spirit </u>(Gal. 3:14). The Holy Spirit dwelling in us is the promise; it is neither financial nor material. In Genesis 12:3, God said that in Him all the families (nations) of the earth would be blessed (salvation). There is a spiritual blessing much greater than the physical land promised to Israel. He promised to give Abraham a heavenly country. Remember the land of Canaan was the physical Promised Land that God promised to Israel, but our promise land is a spiritual kingdom—the kingdom of God. God promised him a heavenly land, not just an earthly land, and that is what Abraham was expecting, not just an earthly Jerusalem. We are going to receive a heavenly Jerusalem, a heavenly country. We may speak about the promise of the Spirit of God as riches, money, wealth, and earthly things, but that is not the case.

Jesus says in His name we are going to cast out demons. Jesus gave us the authority in the New Testament. In His name, so when the devil is messing with our money, we better take the authority in

His name. <u>Do not quote Malachi 3:11 and say the Lord will rebuke the devourer for our sakes.</u> He told that to Israel, because they did not have the name of Jesus. They could not cast the devil out in the name of Jesus. This is our responsibility concerning our finances, our marriage, our health, and in every area of our lives.

We have to stand by faith because Satan will challenge our faith. That is why the Bible says, "Walk by faith, not by sight" (2 Cor. 5:7); it is our responsibility. Which one would we prefer to have: gold, silver (Old Testament money), or the Holy Spirit dwelling in us (New Testament)? Which one would you choose? That's not even a vote. Would we rather have the presence of God living in us or just in our midst, blessing us with riches? NO! The new birth is having the Spirit of God dwelling in us. This is a great mistake of the body of Christ in claiming the promise of the Spirit as financial and material blessings. <u>We are taking away from the glory of Jesus' redemptive work.</u>

Abraham could only receive an earthly (physical) land; however, he saw a heavenly land. This was the great part of Abraham's faith. He was not looking for an earthly land, but that is all God could have given him, because Jesus had not yet come. God dealt with him with material things because no one was born again. They were alive physically, but dead spiritually, separated from God. God made of him a great nation (Israel), blessed him, made his name great (personal), and caused him to be a blessing to others.

What was the blessing that God was speaking about? It was that the Gentiles would come into the kingdom of God and the Spirit of God would dwell within us. When Jesus came, He came as the Lamb of God and the Jews missed it. He is coming back as the Lion of Judah. We believe that the prosperity message taught today is for us today, and <u>we are missing it.</u> We will be judged for our works in heaven (2 Cor. 5:10), and then we will be rewarded. We will reign with Christ, starting with the thousand-year reign and forever.

The *fourth area* is Genesis 12:3: "I will bless them that bless thee and curse him that curseth thee: and in thee shall all families be blessed." *The nations' and people's relationships with Israel will cause them to be either blessed or cursed.*

Genesis 13:2: "And Abram was very rich in cattle, in silver, and in gold" (personal promise). That does not mean we will be very rich. We say that Abraham was very rich, <u>so we claim Abraham's personal blessings.</u> We also believe that the Bible says that the blessings of Abraham will come upon the Gentiles. He was not speaking about material things for us; He was speaking about salvation coming upon all the families of the earth. God said that Abraham would be the father of many nations. *Does that mean that we also will be the father of many nations?* No! Are all the Christians in the world supposed to be rich? No! Jesus said you are going to have the poor always, which includes some Christians (Matt. 26:11). Are we going to call Jesus a liar? Genesis 13:15: "For all the land which thou seest [physically and spiritually], to thee will I give it . . ."

The nation of Israel received the physical land in Abraham because of the covenant of Abraham, Isaac, and Jacob. There is a physical and a spiritual promise being made. In verse 17, God said whatever you see physically, walk through it, and Israel will possess it (physically). Under the Old Testament, God gave the land of Israel to Abraham and to his seed forever. Galatians 3:16 tells us that He was also speaking spiritually. God was speaking about Jesus. Galatians 3:16: "Now to Abraham and his seed were the promises made. He saith not, And to seeds, as of many [people of Israel]; but as of one, And to thy seed, which is Christ."

Both Jews and Gentiles in Christ have a heavenly country. Remember Hebrews 11:10 says Abraham "looked for a city which hath foundations, whose builder and maker is God." Verse 13 says, ". . . they were strangers and pilgrims on the earth." Verse 16 says *they desired a heavenly country.* Genesis 13:16: "And I will make your seed as the dust of the earth [innumerable . . . you will not be able to count the members of the <u>spiritual body of Christ—the true church</u> (Col. 1:18)]: so that if a man can number the dust of the earth, then shall thy seed also be numbered."

God gave Israel an earthly Jerusalem and an earthly country because no one was born again, which is all they could receive. Jesus had not yet died, been neither buried nor raised. We have spiritual blessings that are forever! Galatians 3:16: ". . . He saith not, And to seeds, as of many; but as of one, And to thy seed, which is Christ."

The principal here is for us to get out of the earthly realm and look into the spiritual realm. That is what Abraham did. Genesis 22:17: "That in blessing I will bless thee, and in multiplying I will multiply thy seed [Jesus] as the stars of the heaven, and as the sand which is upon the sea shore; and thy seed shall possess the gate of his enemies." He was not speaking about Israel, as they were conquered most of the time, physically. God was speaking about Jesus. The gates of hell shall not prevail against the church (Matt. 16:18). Verse 19 "And I will give unto thee [church] the keys of the kingdom of heaven . . ." We have the keys spiritually, as He was speaking spiritually.

Today, we spend a lot of time on material and financial things. God was not speaking about these things to us. Genesis 22:18: "And in thy seed shall all the nations of the earth be blessed; because thou hast obeyed my voice." Abraham became the father (spiritually) of all nations, because he trusted God. Everyone was spiritually dead, including Abraham, even though his faith was counted as righteousness. Everyone was spiritually broke, no one had eternal life, not even Abraham, but his faith was counted as righteousness. Hebrews 11:8: "By faith Abraham, when he was called to go out into a place which he should after receive for an inheritance, obeyed and he went out not knowing whither he went." He obeyed!

The number one thing that the body of Christ needs is for us to live a life of obedience, just because we love Him. Simple as that— we love God, and not because we want something. If Adam would have obeyed God, then Jesus would not have died. Obedience is better than sacrifice! Abraham received a physical country and city, Jerusalem, because that is all God could have given him under the Old Testament, but that is not what Abraham was seeking. He knew about the seed to come, because God made the promise to Eve that the seed of the woman was going to crush the serpent's head. That seed is the Messiah, Jesus.

Hebrews 11:9: "By faith he sojourned in the land of promise, as in a strange country, dwelling in tabernacles with Isaac and Jacob." Sojourn means we are just passing through; it is temporary, we are not going to stay. The Bible says sojourning "in the land of promise," the physical land of Israel. Abraham knew that he was just passing through, and so are we. This earth is a strange country for us, we are just passing through. Verse 10: "For he (Abraham) looked for a city which hath foundations, whose builder and maker is God." He was not speaking about an earthly Jerusalem, which men built. He said the builder is God. He was speaking about a heavenly Jerusalem. He was seeing beyond the natural, but he knew that was all he could receive at that time. *The Promised Land (Canaan) was all Israel could receive; a land of milk and honey, financial and material prosperity that fades away.*

Our Promised Land is the kingdom of God, an eternal spiritual kingdom that will never fade away. (Hebrews 8:6 says we have a better covenant [Jesus] established upon better promises than the old covenant.) Hebrews 11:13: "These all died in faith, not having received the promises [Abraham died without having received either the physical or the spiritual promises, but by faith he received them.], but having seen them afar off [he saw them by faith], and were persuaded of them, and embraced them [spiritual—heavenly Jerusalem, heavenly country], and confessed that *they were strangers and pilgrims on this earth.*" Verse 14: "For they that say such things declare plainly that they seek a country." Verse 15: "And truly, if they had been mindful of that country from whence they came out, they might have had opportunity to have returned." Verse 16: "But now they desire a better country, that is, an heavenly . . ." A heavenly country is what Abraham saw by faith; he was not looking for an earthly country, but it is all God could give him. No one could go into heaven without Jesus. He received it by faith, but he did not have the manifestation. Verse 16: "But now they desire a better country, that is, an heavenly: wherefore God is not ashamed to be called their God: for he hath prepared for them a city." Another blessing is the heavenly Jerusalem. In John 14:2, Jesus says, "In my father's house are many mansions . . ." This is neither an earthly city, nor an earthly place for us to dwell, but a heavenly place.

1 Peter 1:17: "And if ye call on the Father, who without respect of persons judgeth according to every man's work, pass the time of your sojourning [your pilgrimage] here in fear." We are just passing through; that is all we are doing. Verse 18: "Forasmuch as ye know that ye were not redeemed with corruptible things, as

silver or gold [which is the standard for money; *the world has been focusing on money from the beginning],* from your vain conversation [lifestyles] received by tradition from your fathers." Verse 19: "But with the precious blood of Christ, as of a lamb without blemish and without spot."

2 Peter 3:10: "But the day of the Lord will come as a thief in the night; in the which the heavens shall pass away with a great noise, and the elements shall melt with fervent heat, the earth also and the works that are therein shall be burned up." Verse 11: "Seeing then that all these things shall be dissolved, what manner of person ought ye to be in all holy conversation [lifestyle] and godliness." In other words, all these things are going to pass away; they are going to burn up. He was telling us that we are just passing through; we are not going to stay on this old earth. In Revelation 21, John spoke about the New Jerusalem, an eternal city, and a new earth. We have to look past what people are telling us. We really have to search the Scriptures over and over again to find the TRUTH!

God promised to dwell in us by His Spirit. He did not promise that He was going to give us a lot of money; that is not Bible. Galatians 3:7: "Know ye therefore that they which are of faith, the same are the children of Abraham." We are the church, whether you were a Jew or Gentile, we that are of faith. Verse 8: "And the scripture, foreseeing that God would justify the heathen through faith, preached before the gospel unto Abraham, saying, In thee shall all nations be blessed." God preached the gospel to Abraham. Verse 14: "That the blessing of Abraham might come upon the Gentiles through Jesus Christ." What blessing? Verse 8 says that God would justify the Gentiles (heathens). Not only the Jews, but also us; this is the blessing of Abraham! God was going to save us, so that all the nations would be blessed and we would become the (spiritual) children of Abraham through Jesus Christ. This is the blessing. *We are all going to have eternal life because of Abraham, not a bunch of money.* Verse 9: "So then they which be of faith are blessed with faithful Abraham," through his seed Jesus.

Jesus redeemed us from the curse of the law, so we are already redeemed. The only problem is that the devil is hanging around harassing us. 1 Timothy 6:12 tells us to fight the good fight of faith.

Abraham, by faith, pleased God, so the devil is trying to tell us to walk by sight and not by faith. Speaking God's Word, the word of faith is the authority we have, quoting the Scriptures. We shouldn't live by what we see or feel. We receive the promise of the Spirit through faith. Through faith the Holy Spirit lives in us; it is called the new birth. That is justifying the heathen. <u>The new birth, being born again, is what God was speaking about.</u> <u>The Holy Ghost living in us.</u> That is the promise of the Spirit. The Bible says God is not a respecter of persons. The Jews could not receive the new birth. They were called God's people under the Old Testament because of the covenant of Abraham.

Paul said, in Romans 3:23, "For all have sinned and come short of the glory of God." Romans 3:10: "As it is written, there is none righteous, no not one." We were all dead in our sins, but the gift of God is eternal life through Jesus. If Jesus was not yet here, how were they going to receive the gift of eternal life? There was no gift until Jesus came. So the promise He made to Abraham was that the Holy Ghost would live in us. Galatians 3:16: "Now to Abraham and his seed were the promises made, He saith not, And to seeds, as of many; but as of one, And to thy seed which is Christ." In Christ we have eternal life; God made that promise to Abraham and to his seed, Jesus.

Where were Isaac and Jacob in the Old Testament? They were in Abraham. The Bible says that even the Levites paid tithes in Abraham (Heb. 7:9). *This was about 430 years earlier, when they paid tithes in Abraham.* Where are we? We are in Jesus Christ. God made the promise to Abraham (Old Testament) and to us in Jesus, the seed (New Testament). John 14:16: "And I will pray the Father, and he shall give you another Comforter, that he may abide with you for ever." The promise of the Spirit to abide in us forever is what Abraham saw; he saw God dwelling in us. Peter spoke of this in Acts 2:33: "Therefore being by the right hand of God exalted, and having received of the Father *the promise of the Holy Ghost,* he hath shed forth this, which ye now see and hear." John 14:16: "And I will pray the Father, and he shall give you another Comforter that he may abide [that means to take up residence and dwell in us] with you for ever." Verse 17: "Even the spirit of truth [the Holy Ghost] <u>whom the</u>

world cannot receive . . ." *The world can receive Jesus when they believe in Him (John 3:16).*

This is the new birth; when the Holy Ghost comes to dwell in us. That is the promise He was speaking about to justify the sinner. John 14:17: ". . . whom the world cannot receive, because it seeth him not, neither knoweth him: but ye know him; for he dwelleth with you [I am with you, that is why the Spirit of God is with you], and shall be in you," being born again. Acts 1:4: "And, being assembled together with them, commanded them that they should not depart from Jerusalem, but wait for the promise." The Holy Spirit is the promise Abraham foresaw, the promise of the Spirit of God.

God said that He shall supply all our need, which means we will be sufficient in all things. Yet Paul says he knows how to hunger and to be abased (to be low, humbled, humiliated). We have an enemy, the devil. Paul went into the cities and preached the gospel, where many believed. He said that he had been caught up to the third heaven and saw things there unspeakable. In spite of all that he saw and did, *Paul still had low points in his life*—they often ran him out of town, they stoned him at Lystra, and, in fact, he was beheaded. He said that he had fought the good fight of faith and there was laid up for him a crown (reward) of righteousness; he had finished his course. He was just a stranger on this earth, so how he died—sleeping or being beheaded—was not important to him because to die was to gain, and to be with Christ.

The <u>key</u> point is that God promised Israel under the Old Testament the Promised Land (physical land) that was filled with milk and honey (material and financial prosperity). That's all they could receive because they were spiritually dead. The seed, Jesus, had not come yet. In the New Testament, for we who are in Christ, God promised a heavenly Jerusalem, a heavenly country (spiritual prosperity). Spiritual prosperity is having the Spirit of God in us forever, being spiritually alive, having the fruit of the Spirit in us, and having the glory of God in us. The law was given by Moses, but <u>grace and truth</u> came by Jesus Christ.

CHAPTER 13

Truth # 12:

We Give Willingly to God Because
He First Loved Us and We Love Him

The Bible reveals that, after the rapture of the church, the believers' works are going to be judged, and we will be rewarded every man according to his works. What employer pays his employees before they work? Think about that! Some are preaching that we all can become millionaires today; *this is not a promise of God*. Some Christians become disappointed and get discouraged because they never become rich. *God never promised that every Christian was going to become wealthy.*

There will be *some* Christians who will become wealthy, because they have the *ability* to deal with money wisely. Romans 12:6, 8 say others because of gifts according to the grace of God are going to be blessed with financial riches so that they may give with simplicity unto the kingdom of God. They have a special gift of God. We can't just say, "I want to have money, so that's my calling." No one can say, "I want to be an apostle." The Bible says some are called by God to be apostles. There will be *some* who will prosper because they *manipulate* people. However, God did promise to meet all our need.

This is the best of all the "Twelve Truths," and the key to giving is as simple as this: God wants us to give because we love Him. *God's willingness gave Jesus because He loves us, not because someone commanded Him. Period, the end!* This is not debatable, God is love; it is so simple yet we are so far away in our understanding. We are not commanded to give tithes under the New Testament, but to give to God willingly with a cheerful heart of love. Everything concerning the kingdom of God and our relationship with Jesus is because of love. That's how it started, that's how it is now, and that's how it's going to be forever.

In our understanding, we are so far away from the truth—it's like we are living in some type of twilight zone. Some are focusing on materialistic, financial things, and they are moving parallel with the truth, which is the love of God. One is temporary and the other is eternal; these seem so close, yet they are so far away. The fine line of deception is to focus on the natural above the spiritual. When we understand this, we will see that <u>the whole point of the kingdom of God is love, and God wants us to love Him willingly and freely</u>.

We worship God, we praise Him, we thank Him, and we give to His work because He first loved us. So we show forth our love toward Him with His love that He shed into our hearts by His Spirit (Romans 5:5). We worship God because He is God; that's why we worship Him! He gave us a free will, so we use that free will to love Him and to honor Him. Notice, I said free will. *The Bible says as a man purposes in his heart* (2 Cor. 9:7). We can accept Him (eternal life) or reject Him (eternal damnation). When we accept Jesus, God gives us a new heart and a new spirit filled with His love. The truth is right in front of us, and it's staring us in the face.

We all say that John 3:16 is the greatest verse in the Bible. Everything Jesus did for us was because He loved us. John 3:16: "<u>For God so loved the world, that he gave his only begotten Son</u> . . ." This is the key to the kingdom of God, not us walking around saying we claim this or that. We speak about the kingdom's principles and deep stuff; this is as deep as one can get in God's eyes. There is nothing deeper than truly walking in the love of God, and, if we are honest, none of us come close. *Let us not deceive ourselves; this will definitely take a work of the Holy Spirit.* 1 John 4: 8 says that God is love; it doesn't say God is faith, neither does it say that God is hope, nor that God is wisdom. Romans 5: 5 says His love is shed abroad in our hearts by the Holy Spirit when we receive Jesus. God's love will never leave nor forsake a person, but human love will. God's love bears all things, it is kind, and *it never gives up* (read 1 Cor. 13).

We used to speak about Christians selling chicken dinners for the kingdom of God, to have money for the church. Today, it's just a little more intellectual. Many will say, "Send in your best offering (money) with your prayer cloth." Not once in the New Testament is money mentioned when someone had a need to be healed. *Jesus healed out of compassion and love; the Father met people's need.* You see how far we have gone away from operating in the truth. For God so *loved* the world that He *gave* His only begotten Son.

Romans 10:9 says "that if thou shalt confess with thy mouth the Lord Jesus and shalt believe in thine heart that God hath raised him from the dead, thou shalt be saved;" it has to be from the *heart,* not from the *mind.* The Bible also tells us that God sent not His Son into the world to condemn the world, but that the world, through Jesus, might be saved because of His love (John 3:17). God wants us to return His love back to Him.

We are not commanded to give tithes in the New Testament, but we should give willingly to prove the sincerity of our love (2 Cor. 8:8). *I choose to give tithes and offerings because I take great joy in working with the Holy Spirit,* helping to build the kingdom of God. 2 Corinthians 9:6 says if we sow sparingly, we will reap sparingly, and if we sow bountifully, we will also reap bountifully (literally "with blessings"). God gives us the freedom to give; but Paul says for us not to use our liberty to serve the lust of the flesh. I'm free, so I'm going to keep my money and spend it on myself; that's the lust of the flesh! God wants us to give willingly, as we purpose in our hearts, not out of necessity, for God loves a cheerful giver (2 Cor. 9:7). 1 Corinthians 13:13: "And now abideth faith, hope, charity, these three; but the greatest of these is charity" (God's love). This is the key to the kingdom of God. We have the key, and we think that it is more finances that we need in order to spread the gospel.

In the early days, it wasn't the money, but the anointing of the Holy Spirit that caused the church to grow. When the church truly walks in the love of God, we will come into unity of the Spirit, and that's when the gospel will be spread throughout the entire world, according to the perfect will of God. Jesus said that all the law and prophets (Old Testament) is fulfilled through love. Love doesn't want to cause anyone pain.

One of the problems we have today is that husbands and wives cause each other pain. We get married, and we cause each other pain; isn't that dumb? *Christians cause pain to other Christians by criticizing, gossiping, forsaking, and not forgiving one another.* When we say we forgive someone, but we just won't fellowship with them; as though Jesus would forgive us and not fellowship with us forever. <u>We truly haven't forgiven anyone; we are deceiving ourselves; this is another gospel and not the gospel of Jesus</u>. So quit playing games! 1 John 4:7: "Beloved, let us love one another": this is the very heart of God.

In the church, Christians mock those who sell chicken dinners, have barbeques, and hold rummage sales. Jesus died for all of us, so who are we to judge each other? Romans 14:3,4 says that we are not to judge another, for God has received him. *This is not the heart of God.* God loves him, and Christ died for him. "For love is of God; and everyone that loveth is born of God, and knoweth God." Verse 8 of 1 John 4: "He that loveth not knoweth not God; for God is love." *God manifested His love toward us while we were yet sinners; Jesus died for us.*

We show our love for God through our worship, praise, thanksgiving, our giving freely of tithes and offerings, studying His Word, and fellowshipping with Him from the heart. 1 John 4:17 says, "Herein is our love made perfect, that we have boldness in the day of judgment: because <u>as he [Jesus] is, so are we in this world.</u>" Now we are as Jesus is (spiritually); He was not trying to manipulate people in order to get a large offering, nor should we. Verse 18: "There is no fear in love; but perfect love casteth out fear . . ." We are not commanded to tithe in the New Testament, so when someone tells us that we are under a curse if we don't tithe, they are trying to put fear into us.

In fact, if you do tithe according to Malachi 3:8-10, you are trying to operate under the curse of the law. Paul says, in Galatians 3:10, *"For as many as are of the <u>works of the law are under the curse:</u> for it is written, Cursed is every one that <u>continueth not in all</u>*

things [100 percent] which are written in the book of the law to do them" (See James 2:10, Deut. 28:15, 58). In John 7:19, Jesus says, ". . . none of you keepeth the law . . ." *Jesus has redeemed us from the curse of the law (Gal. 3:13); and if the Son has made us free, then we are free indeed.* Abraham and Jacob were not commanded to tithe; however, under the law of Moses, Israel was (Heb. 7:5). I truly believe that most ministers and believers are honestly ignorant of this fact; however, some willfully don't want us to know this and God will judge them.

Some believers will use their liberty to serve the lust of the flesh and sow sparingly. Pastors' fear says, "Our tithes and offerings are fifty thousand dollars a month; if we tell the people the truth, then our finances might drop to under forty thousand a month." I once heard a preacher, whom I still admire, say about another preacher, "If he keeps preaching that, God is going to dry up his finances." Wrong! We need to preach the truth; God is not going to dry up our finances. Selfishness, the lust of the flesh, and the devil will try to dry up our finances.

Jesus said that if we continue in His Word, we will know the truth and the truth will set us free. *When I give tithes and offerings, I do it willingly, cheerfully, as I purpose in my heart.* Fear will cause some ministers not to tell you the truth, and that's sad; God will hold them accountable in the day of judgment. Some, if they need a million dollars for a certain project, will ask for it, which is good; but once they obtain their goal, they won't tell you that they have enough. They will tell you to keep giving and giving until they have three million. Perhaps you cannot pay your rent or your bills, so now you are angry with God and have stopped going to church. Return to church; it's more important to be in the will of God! Jesus said many that (think they) are first are going to be last, and many that (think they) are last will be first.

In Acts 16, there was a young girl possessed with a demon saying that Paul and Silas showed the way unto God, and that's exactly what they were doing. But Paul, being grieved, cast the spirit of divination out from her; we would think that Paul would have said to her, "Come with us." This young girl was operating under the power of Satan. Paul did not allow her to keep witnessing for Jesus, because behind her was an evil spirit. Had <u>he ignored this,</u> the people would have continued to believe that this was of God, giving the little girl glory while accepting the words that she spoke. When Paul and Silas left, the people would have been deceived.

We grieve the Holy Ghost when <u>we ignore the truth</u> that God has revealed to us. *The fear of losing people and finances causes ministers and churches not to change when they are wrong.* Perfect love casteth out fear because fear has torment. If we want to grow in love, we cannot operate in fear. That's the way we grow toward perfection in love. We are already perfect in Christ (He is our perfection), but if we want to grow, we cannot allow fear to control us.

Galatians 5:22 says that the fruit of the Spirit is love, and Romans 5:5 says ". . . the love of God is shed abroad in our hearts by the Holy Spirit." God's love flows into our hearts by His Spirit when we accept Jesus as our Savior, who dwells in us. 1 Corinthians 13:13: "And now abided faith, hope, charity, these three; but <u>the greatest of these is charity" (God's love).</u> The apostle Paul said by the Spirit of God that love is the greatest. True love comes only from God; He loves us willingly, the same way I want my wife to love me willingly, cheerfully, and from her heart. Do we believe that God wants anything less? Think about it; do you think I want her to love me because I command her?

Even though Jesus commands us to love one another and to love God, He wants us to do it by choice, willingly, from our hearts from a motive of love, honor, and thanksgiving. *Love is the only thing we can never pay out; we always owe love to each other.* We have the love of God in our hearts, so it is possible to love others. If two people in a marriage would learn to love each other with the love of God (willingly by choice) instead of trying to command each other, then their marriage would succeed.

In 2 Corinthians 8:7, Paul says, "Therefore, as ye abound in every thing, in faith, and utterance, and knowledge, in all diligence, and in your love to us, see that *ye abound in this grace* also." He was speaking about our giving as grace; it is God's grace that allows us to give to His work. Did you know that? God wants us to give by His grace and not by commandment. Verse 8: "I speak not by commandment but by occasion of the forwardness of others, and <u>to prove the</u>

sincerity of your love." 2 Corinthians 8 reveals to us that we are not commanded by God to give our finances to Him; otherwise, He would be making us robots.

Grace is not a burden; God allows us to be a worker together with the Holy Ghost (2 Cor. 6:1). We are workers together with the Holy Ghost to build His kingdom; this is the grace of God. God could have done it without us, but He chose to include us through preaching and witnessing. Whatever it is that God wants us to do, *we should do it willingly from a heart of love.* Paul spoke not by commandment (this is not a commandment); he's telling us that we should abound in this grace—giving. The word "forwardness" means earnestness. He was speaking about others—they were diligent; they were eager to give. He was saying, "I'm not commanding you to give, but I want you to abound in this grace also; in other words, show your sincerity of your love for God by your giving." This is not a commandment of God, but the way you abound in knowledge, utterance, faith, diligence, and love, see that you abound in the grace of giving also.

Jesus proved His love for us by dying for our sins. Verse 9 of 2 Corinthians chapter 8 says, "For ye know the grace of our Lord Jesus Christ, that, though he was rich, yet for your sakes he became poor, that ye through his poverty might be rich." Jesus left the glory of heaven, came down to this sin-corrupt earth, died for us, and *made us rich with eternal life—something no one had ever done. Men already had financial and material wealth.*

Hebrews 7:5 says, "And verily they that are of the sons of Levi . . ." The Levites, who had the priesthood, were commanded to take tithes from the people, according to the law. We are not under the law, but under grace; Jesus fulfilled all the law for us. Verse 18: "For there is verily a disannulling [to put away] of the commandment going before for the weakness and unprofitableness thereof." The law made nothing perfect but the bringing in of a better hope. Jesus made us perfect in Him! The Levites were commanded to take tithes of the people, but we are not under the law after He has redeemed us.

Acts 2:1 is truly the beginning of the New Testament. *The four gospels took place under the Old Testament, although they are listed in the New Testament. Jesus lived under the Old Testament, and He brought us a better covenant (New Testament) after He ascended into heaven.* Galatians 4:4 says that Jesus was born of a woman (Mary) "made under the law." Galatians 4:5 says, "To redeem them that were under the law . . ." The law was until the seed came (Gal. 3:19), which means until Jesus came, died, was buried, resurrected, ascended on high, and sent the Holy Ghost.

In the New Testament, there are only six verses that speak of tithes. Hebrews 7:2 says, "To whom also Abraham gave a tenth part of all . . ." Verse 4 says Abraham gave a tenth of the spoils; verse 5 says that the sons of <u>Levi had a commandment to take tithes of the people, according to the law of Moses.</u> Verse 6 says Melchisedec received tithes of Abraham. Verse 8 says, "And <u>here</u> men [Levites on earth] that died receive tithes; but <u>there</u> he [Jesus in heaven] receiveth them, of whom it is *witnessed that he liveth."* Verse 9 says, ". . . Levi, also who received tithes, paid tithes in Abraham." *There are 3,816 verses in the New Testament, and tithing is mentioned only six times, and five of those are quotes from the Old Testament. Only half of Hebrews 7:8 speaks of tithing in the New Testament.*

When the Old Testament spoke about Abraham tithing to Melchisedec, this was not the issue. It was speaking about Jesus, after the similitude of Melchisedec, having a greater priesthood then the Levitical priesthood. The focus was not about tithing. If tithing was of the New Testament, don't you believe there would be more than half a verse out of 3,816 verses? How much preaching do we hear today on tithing? We hear a lot! Paul (by the Holy Spirit) told us to prove our love for God by giving, even though we are not commanded. We hear a lot about Malachi 3:8-10; it is preached all the time. Yes, I believe in giving more than a tithe, because I have a *better covenant.* The difference is *I choose to give out of love.*

We have the Scriptures, and yet we are so far away from the truth of God at times. Malachi 3:8 says, "Will a man rob God?" Why was God saying *to Israel,* "Will a man rob me?" The people of Israel were commanded to pay tithes under the law of Moses. If they didn't tithe, they would have been operating under a curse. Malachi 3:9: "Ye are cursed with a curse: for ye have robbed me, even *this* whole *nation" (Israel).* Galatians 3:13 says Christ has redeemed us from the curse of the law. If Israel tithed, they were blessed; likewise, if we tithe, we are blessed. If Israel didn't tithe, they were cursed. <u>If when we don't tithe we are under a curse, then what did Jesus redeem us from, if we are still under a curse by not tithing?</u> What is the difference between the church (after Jesus) and Israel (before Jesus) if we are still under a curse?

The Bible, God's Word, says, "Christ hath redeemed us from the curse of the law, being made a curse for us . . ." (Gal. 3:13). Galatians 5:14 says, "For <u>all the law</u> is fulfilled in one word . . ." *The word is "love"; Jesus loves us. And in Christ, no one can put us back under the curse.* John 8:36 says, "If the Son shall make you free, ye shall be free indeed." Paul says in Galatians 3:3, "Are ye so foolish? having begun in the Spirit [free from the law], are ye now made perfect by the flesh [works of the law]?" Malachi 3:8-10 is in the Old Testament and under the law of Moses. Abraham tithed because he reverenced and loved God, not because he was commanded, the same as we should do today. He was not, nor was Jacob, under a curse. *Please study this carefully and humbly. Pray and ask God to give us revelation concerning this matter.* <u>When we tithe under the Old Testament (law) we are trying to take away from the glory of Jesus' death, burial, and resurrection—His work at the cross.</u> He did it all (100 percent) for us. John 19:30 says, *". . . It is finished."* Jesus fulfilled all the law for us.

Abraham sought a heavenly country, a heavenly city; he also believed God was able to raise Isaac from the dead, but under the Old Testament all he could receive were material and financial blessings. Hebrews 11:39 says: ". . . all having obtained a good report through faith received not the promise." Abraham died without receiving the promise, the physical land of Canaan and the spiritual land, the kingdom of God; he died in faith. Abraham was looking for a city made by God. *He had a vision, and he tithed out of the love he had for God.* God neither commanded Abraham to give tithes, nor did he command Jacob to give tithes.

Malachi 3:10: "Bring ye all the tithes into the storehouse . . ." That's a commandment of the Old Testament under the law of Moses; they were supposed to bring the tithes into the storehouse, because <u>God commanded the sons of Levi to take tithes of the people according to the law (Heb. 7:8).</u> Many Christians still try to live under the Old

Testament; for example, they say the Lord will rebuke the devourer for our sakes. Wrong!

In the New Testament, God will not rebuke the devourer; He commands us to cast out demons in His name. Jesus said in His name we are to bind the devil. Whatsoever we bind on earth shall be bound in heaven, and whatsoever we loose on earth shall be loosed in heaven. He gave us the authority to tread over serpents and scorpions and over all the power of the enemy, and nothing by any means shall (truly) harm us. They killed Paul, and some will say that God's Word is not true because he said that nothing by any means will hurt them. He was speaking to his disciples, including Peter, John and James; they all were martyred, except John. *They truly cannot harm us*. We can die physically, but Jesus was speaking about something far greater than physical life—eternal life.

In John 8:56, Jesus revealed that Abraham was looking much further than what we think. Jesus said, "Your father Abraham rejoiced to see my day: and he saw it, and was glad" (John 8:56). Not only did Abraham see a heavenly Jerusalem and country, he even saw the day of Jesus; he saw a lot further than his physical descendents possessing the land of Canaan. Abraham believed God was able to raise Isaac from the dead.

In 2 Corinthians 8:24, Paul told the Corinthians to show proof of the sincerity of their love. God manifested His love towards us by sending Jesus to redeem us; this is the proof of His love. *God gave because He loved us; we should give to God's work because we love Him*. Paul says the proof of our love is giving not by commandment but by love. Chapter 8, verse 12, of 2 Corinthians: "For if there be first a willing mind . . ." Does this sound like a commandment? If you are commanded, you may or may not be willing. If I said to my wife, "I command you to kiss me," she just might smack me on the head, but if she just walked up and kissed me, I would say "What's that for?" She would say, "I'm just glad to be married to you." She did that, and it was a million times better.

The law of Christ is the law of love, and we give by the grace of God. In 2 Corinthians 8:7, Paul says to see that we abound in this grace also. It is by the grace of God that we are allowed to give into His work. John 1:17: "For the law was given by Moses, but grace and truth came by Jesus Christ." 2 Corinthians 9:6: "But this I say, He which soweth sparingly shall reap also sparingly [you give little, you reap little]; and he which soweth bountifully shall reap also bountifully." This literally means "with blessings." You will be blessed. Verse 7: "Every man according as he purposeth in his heart . . ." Personally, I purpose to give more than 10 percent. Under the law, we would be cursed with a curse if we gave 8 percent; however, under grace, God says as we purpose in our hearts. Our giving shows the sincerity of our love; <u>the key to everything is love.</u>

A person who loves God will follow Him after a life of obedience and holiness. According to the degree we obey, God demonstrates how much we love Him. Jesus said he that loves me will keep my commandments. He was not speaking about the Ten Commandments; He was speaking about everything that He had said in His Word. Jesus also said he who loves me will keep my Word. Every man according as he purposes in his heart, so let him give: that means you make a choice. 2 Corinthians 8:12 says let there be "<u>first a willing mind,</u>" so that you will give as God directs you.

Preachers sometimes press people to give more by saying, "Give a little more, sister, a little more, brother. The Lord wants you to give a thousand dollars and

He is going to give you a hundredfold return this year." Quit it! This is not the work of God, but of men! We criticize other churches when they don't measure up to our expectations about what the Bible says. Jesus died for them; we didn't. We are so far away from what God really wants us to do; although *we say that we are faith people, we need to be people of love, which is far greater.*

Every man according to the purpose in his heart: that means he makes a decision, so let him give not grudgingly. We should not let anyone manipulate us. They will say that we are cheap (guilt trip), we are cursed (fear). "God will bless you with 100 percent return now (thousand-year reign); send $100 with your prayer request or prayer cloth (<u>not once in the New Testament).</u>" Jesus died for all of mankind and never charged a single person for His salvation, nor did He ever mention money to them for any type of deliverance. Isaiah 55:1 says, "Ho, every one that thirsteth, come ye to the waters, and he that hath <u>no money;</u> come ye, buy, and eat; yea, come, buy wine and milk <u>without money and without price"</u> (salvation, healings, and deliverance)."

Hebrews 6:10: "For God is not unrighteous to forget your work and labour of love, which ye have shewed toward his name, and that ye have ministered to the saints and do minister." They were giving their finances to the poor saints, which showed forth a labor of love. Giving is a labor of love. When we give to the poor, it's called a labor of love because it takes an effort for us to earn the money and then give it away. Jesus showed forth His labor of love by dying for us. 2 John 5:6 speaks about God's plan for our lives; it is for us to walk in love in every area of our lives, to be a blessing to people, and to truly love one another.

Love will never leave us nor forsake us, it will speak the truth and correct us, and it will never give up on us. Jesus is our example, and He never gives up on us. Love will cause us to give our lives, our finances, and ourselves for others; it gives us great joy. That's why in Acts 20:35 Paul reminds us that Jesus said it is more blessed to give than to receive, as it will bring us joy. *The law of Christ is the law of love and freedom; it is the law of liberty;* we have been called unto liberty, not to serve the flesh, but to love one another. This is the very heart of God, the law of Christ. Everything we do should be motivated by love, and this is the love that we walk after His word. God doesn't command us on how much we should give to the poor or how much we should give in the offering.

<u>The law of Christ is a royal law; it's a law of freedom, a law of liberty; it is the law of love.</u> The law of Moses commanded Israel to tithe, but the law of Christ comes from the heart, and not from tables of stones. The parallel lines or the twilight zone lines of the Scriptures are as close as one can get between the truth and error. We give to God for the growth of the ministry, so that the kingdom of God can be enlarged, by people being saved, believers being taught God's Word, and living the life of Christ as much as possible. James 2:8 says, "If ye fulfil <u>the royal law</u> according to the scripture, Thou shalt love thy neighbor as thyself, ye do well." Look at verse 12: "So speak ye, and so do, as they that shall be judged by the law of liberty" (freedom).

You are free in Christ Jesus. In John 8:31, Jesus said, "If ye continue in my word, then are ye my disciples indeed." Verse 32: "And ye shall know the truth, and the truth shall make you free." Verse 36: "If the Son therefore shall make you free, ye shall be free indeed." God has set us free; <u>do not allow anyone to deceive you and put you back into bondage</u>. *The Bible says you will suffer if a man puts you in bondage (2 Cor. 11:20).* If a man manipulates you or if someone puts burdens on you, that is what men's religion will do. James 2:10: "For whosoever shall keep the whole law [Mosaic Law] and yet offend in one point, <u>he is guilty of all</u> [the whole law]." Verse 11 speaks of adultery and killing. Verse 12: "So speak ye, and so do, as they that shall be judged by the law of liberty." The law of freedom, the law of love, that's how we want to be judged and not by the law of Moses.

The <u>key</u> point is that we are not commanded in the New Testament to give tithes, we are to give willingly as we purpose in our hearts, and our motive must be love. We are not to use our liberty in Christ to serve the lust of the flesh, by living for self and not for Christ. *Many are looking for some deep revelation, and we are missing the greatest revelation of all.* Everything that we do for God should be out of love and for His glory, including our giving. We have God's love within us. Romans 13:10: "<u>Therefore love is the fulfilling of the law.</u>" Consequently, we should love God and each other the same as God loves us.

CHAPTER 14

A Fresh and Honest Study of the Bible

W e all need to be open for correction and ready to repent (change) when we miss the mark of the Scriptures. Today the "Truth Church" (the spiritual body of Christ that the Holy Spirit, not man, baptizes us into when we truly accept Jesus as our Savior—1ˢᵗ Cor. 12:12-14; Titus 3:5) is divided because of pride. There are many denominations and nondenominational churches that have followed men placing them above the Scriptures. They will not fellowship with each other, using *their church doctrine of belief to stay separated, believing that they have the whole truth, when really none of us do*. This is not accepted to God because Paul writes, "is Christ divided?" (1 Cor. 1:13). No! The truth must be based on the Scriptures alone, after studying with prayer and being willing to change when in error. I did, and I ate humble pie.

Instead of criticizing each other, we could have certain *Bible-knowledgeable men and women come together in their own denominations and nondenominational churches to fast, pray, and study the Bible*. We could with an honest heart seek God to reveal to us His truth and to help us change our belief, so that we will line up with the *Scriptures*. We, the truth church—the spiritual body of Christ—may not agree 100 percent on everything. However, if we truly seek God, the space of disagreement will be a lot smaller. We need to do a fresh study of the Scriptures and stop pretending that we have it all together; Jesus was and still is the only perfect one. Possibly we could go from 70 percent (symbolic) agreement to a 95 percent (symbolic) agreement, within the whole of the church, based on what the Bible truly teaches.

Concerning this book, the Holy Spirit revealed that there will be four categorized groups of readers: The <u>first group</u> is the Christians readers who have no belief concerning financial or spiritual prosperity, *not knowing the Scriptures*. This book will be a blessing to them, causing them to seek the face of God and not His hand. The <u>second group</u> is those who already believe that true prosperity was spiritual, but *knew only a few scriptures* to prove their belief. This book will give them an abundance of scriptures. The <u>third group</u> is those who believe, like I did, that Jesus came to give us eternal life with an abundance of material and financial prosperity. After reading and studying the abundance of scriptures (100 percent Bible) in these twelve truths, *they will repent like I did* and recognize that Jesus came to give us spiritual prosperity and not financial things. The <u>fourth group</u> is those *who will hold to their belief,* in spite of what the Scriptures say, because of pride and the fear of man, and some truly will not receive the revelation. *In Mark 7:13, Jesus warns us about making the Word of God of no effect by our own traditions.* Remember God knows the heart, and we will all stand before the judgment seat of Christ.

Index

Prayer for Salvation

Lord Jesus, I know that I am a sinner and there is absolutely nothing I can do to save myself, so I am coming to You to ask You to save me. I put my trust in You 100 percent, asking You to save and cleanse me from all of my sins. So right now, I confess You as my Lord, and I receive You as my Savior because I believe in my heart that You died for my sins and that You were raised from the dead so that I can have eternal life in You. I thank You, Lord Jesus, for saving me. Amen.

Your next step is to be baptized in water. Also, attend a good Bible-teaching church that focuses on loving God and one another, living for Jesus, and not money.

Allen J. Charbonnet is co-founder and pastor of the Word of God Ministries Church in Long Beach, California, a church of many races. He accepted the Lord and was spirit-filled on April 30, 1975, a Wednesday night, in the city of Carson, California. God poured out four miracles (God's sovereign grace) upon him that night. God called him into the ministry as a New Testament teacher, according to 1 Corinthians 12:28: "And God hath set some in the church, first apostles, secondarily prophets, thirdly teachers . . ." He reads and studies the Word of God in detail, almost every day, checking the Bible to see that which he sees and hears is scriptural.

How to contact the author:
Write: Pastor Allen Charbonnet, Word of God Ministries, PO Box 4595, Cerritos, California 90703

Visit: 1401 West Spring Street, Long Beach, California 90810

E-mail: pastorcharbonnet@netscape.net

Website: wordofgodministrieschurch.com

Printed in the United States
62792LVS00002B/1-186

9 781600 344947